PRAISE FOR *THE BETTER COLLEGE ESSAY*

"For many students, the college admission essay is the most daunting part of applying to college. Elizabeth Stone draws upon her extensive experience guiding students through all aspects of the admission process to show parents, teachers, counselors, and others how to effectively mentor students as they tackle their essays. Chock full of great tips and sample essays, *The Better College Essay* is a resource that will prove invaluable for anyone wanting to help teenagers present themselves authentically and distinctively."

— *Sally P. Springer, Ph.D.*
Associate Chancellor Emerita, UC Davis
Co-author, Admission Matters: What Students and Parents Need to Know About
Getting Into College

"*The Better College Essay* is an excellent resource for students and writing mentors looking to demystify the college essay writing process. Elizabeth Stone does a stellar job of explaining the purpose of the college essay, breaking down the process of writing it into manageable parts and providing many sample essay prompts and drafts of real college essays. Most important, Stone understands the importance of nurturing students' authentic voices in their college essays so that they can remain true to themselves, write the best essays that they can, and appeal to the college that is right for them. I plan to use some of Stone's sound advice in my eleventh-grade English classes when my students tremble at the thought of writing mock college essays in preparation for senior year."

—*Lori D'Amico*
English Teacher
Hunter College High School, New York City

"Elizabeth Stone has written a clear, helpful book with an important and somewhat unique twist. Most books about college admission essay writing are for students and parents, and many are extremely useful. But this one is different; it is written for advisors and teachers who are charged with the mission of helping students write college essays. It is an engaging book written for adults. Dr. Stone's approach is measured and easy to follow as she outlines and illustrates a reasonable step-by-step approach for instructors to use as they guide their young students through the college essay-writing process. Her focus is not on a wholesale re-crafting of an essay but, rather, on improving it incrementally with hints on how to make each word more valuable and how to enrich the content of every paragraph. She avoids 'educationalese' jargon and theory and focuses on the re___ ___ ___ writing for the limited purpose of creating an interesting essay that will shed light on the ___ ___ ___ ___ strengths in a way that may enhance the probability of getting the ___ ___ ___ ge of choice. Dr. Stone's book belongs in the library of ever ___ ___ ople successfully navigate the increasingly daunting water ___

___ *Ph.D.*
Former Principal, Gunn High School, Palo Alto, California

"Finally! A book written for counselors and advisors working with students through the college essay process. Many books are written for students on how to write a good college essay. Now counselors and advisors have their own 'how-to' manual. Identifying essay types, complete with examples and suggestions, provides a needed tool for advisors. Chock full of examples, guidelines, recommendations, and more, this book will quickly become a classic resource every counselor will reach for on their shelves, to use as they guide students through the daunting college essay process. Elizabeth Stone has written an easy-to-follow book for college counselors to use to not only guide, but to push students beyond their comfort zones when writing. Elizabeth writes, 'Greatness often comes with collaboration and partnership . . . working with someone who pushes your perceived limits.' Elizabeth gives a roadmap for helping students to use the college essay process as an integral part of their self-exploration, as they prepare to move from high school to college. This book will be dog-eared by the end of this summer. I plan to use it that much in my work with students."

—*Cyndy McDonald*
Founder, Higher Education Consultants Association
Founder, GuidedPath

"In this book, Elizabeth captures the essential truth: it doesn't really matter whether your essay is about gummi worms, a Supreme Court justice, or dance rehearsals; it's about sharing an essential and authentic piece of yourself. She not only shows the way and uses dozens of examples to illustrate, but provides guidance to students and counselors and mentors alike that can make the entire process meaningful to the student. The book is creatively constructed and invaluable as it takes the terrifying and anxiety-provoking essay and explains its point, the types, and the mission and guides the process. I'll use its lessons in my own writing."

—*Mark H. Sklarow*
Chief Executive Officer, Independent Educational Consultants Association

"As an academic coach who works with teens who are often challenged by the mere thought of constructing an essay of any sort, I am delighted by Elizabeth Stone's engaging how-to manual on creating the college admission essay. Elizabeth's insider knowledge of the college admission process makes her an invaluable guide through the daunting essay-writing process. I look forward to implementing her savvy and creative techniques for helping students craft an essay that best represents them."

—*Beth Samuelson*
Director, SOS 4 Students

The Better College Essay: Fitting In *and* Standing Out

ELIZABETH A. STONE, Ph.D.

Foreword by Douglas L. Christiansen, Ph.D.
Vice Provost for Enrollment and Dean of Admissions, Vanderbilt University

WINTERGREEN ORCHARD HOUSE • WESTFORD, MASSACHUSETTS

Editorial Note

The essay examples included in this book may contain some grammatical, punctuation, and other stylistic errors. The author and the book's editors have chosen to retain these errors in an effort to accurately represent the students' writing and to demonstrate the process of guiding college applicants from the first to final drafts of their essays.

A Wintergreen Orchard House Book
Published by Wintergreen Orchard House.

© 2014 by Elizabeth A. Stone, Ph.D.

Wintergreen Orchard House is a division of Carnegie Communications.

ISBN: 978-1-936035-75-5

Book design by NOON SF
Author photograph by Sam Maller

Manufactured in the United States of America

Wintergreen Orchard House
2 LAN Drive, Suite 100, Westford, MA 01886
Tel: 978-692-2747 FAX: 978-692-2304
info@wintergreenorchardhouse.com
www.WintergreenOrchardHouse.com

To David and Janet

CONTENTS

In the holistic college admission process of today, the college essay plays a critical role in the admission decision. Why is the essay so important and why will reading *The Better College Essay: Fitting In* and *Standing Out* possibly make a difference in the process? Dr. Elizabeth Stone has crafted an excellent resource to help mentors understand the answers to these questions. Simply put, the college essay is the student's one chance to let the admission officer or committee hear his or her voice. Additionally, this resource will help mentors understand the criticality of why it is imperative the individual student stand out. When all other variables are equal—meaning test scores, grades, class rank, rigor of course work, excellent recommendation letters, leadership, and extracurricular activities—the essay may be the defining piece.

With twenty-seven years of experience in higher education, and as an expert in enrollment management and college admission, I know this book will be helpful to those who mentor students as they navigate the complex path of the college admission process. The holistic admission process takes all components of an application into consideration, not just test scores and grades. In the essay, the student pulls back the curtain of his or her mind, allowing the reader a peek into some aspect of the student's life, feelings, and experiences. Through this brief encounter, the student reveals such things as the ability to think abstractly, deeply, and thoughtfully regarding a subject. It may also explain why an incident in life has been a catalyst for growth and development, many times life-altering and to the betterment of that student's corner of the world. Admission officers want to know, when students have unique experiences, what happened next as a result of those experiences? How was the student changed? What did the student do to make a difference in his or her life going forward? Additionally, the essay allows those who read it to imagine the student speaking directly to them, in their voice, thus letting the reader feel and understand the passion, pain, joy, or victory being written about. Dr. Stone's book speaks to ways to empower students to create that voice and let the reader gain true insight through a well thought-out and executed essay.

The critical point of the book, while geared toward mentors of students, is that the essay must be the student's work and in the student's voice. Parents, teachers, and mentors have always offered advice on the essay, but it is the student's voice that must be heard, and the student must always have the freedom to use that voice. It is a fine line that someone offering a critical review of the essay walks, and Dr. Stone has successfully defined that role and its importance in the process. The tools she has included, such as the parental and student questionnaires, are excellent resources to get conversations started. She has also stressed the necessity of allowing students the freedom to follow their own instincts and creativity when choosing the subject of the essay, and then in the writing itself.

Mentors of this process are just that: mentors. However, when dealing with adolescents, it may feel that the role is more that of a trail guide, or the adult with the flashlight when the electricity goes off. As a mentor, providing gentle guidance for the students, helping them when they lose their way—but not telling them which path to take, which words to use, what experience to write about—is the key. Dr. Stone is clear and concise in her guidance, and through her own experiences with her two daughters, reveals that her personal experiences as well as those with students she has mentored have led to the creation of this excellent guide. No two students have the same experiences. Students bring their unique gifts to the table, and it is the wise mentor who learns to listen before guiding. Dr. Stone's insights and tools will assist mentors on this journey.

Having spent her career in the study of adolescence, educating others on child and adolescent development, and now mentoring students through the admission process, Dr. Stone is an expert in her field. Her words of wisdom will guide everyone, from a first-time mentor or parent helping their first child through the process, to a seasoned veteran, offering assistance and a critical eye to the essay writer. Dr. Stone's suggestions— such as "editing without a pen," meaning, having the student take a step back and give a passage additional thought for word choice—are a simple way to explain the difficult task of rewriting the essay after the first draft.

Many times, the mentor is someone very close to the student—a parent, relative, best friend's parent, favorite teacher, or personal mentor such as scout leader. Because the mentor knows the student well, it may be more difficult to detach emotionally while mentoring. This book guides you through the process of stepping back and detaching for the betterment of the process. Students in high school are passionate about life and their experiences. That passionate voice is what makes the better essay, what makes the essay stand out, and what leads admission officers to gain a deeper sense of the student.

Dr. Stone's book will help the mentor ascertain whether the writer is on-mark for the type of essay requested by the college or university. Her clear definitions and concise examples will be very valuable when working with students. Additionally, her mantras of authenticity and the essay being the student's own work and in his or her own voice add great credibility to this work. As a dean of admissions for many years, let me clearly state that if an essay is not the student's work, the admission officers will know that immediately. And, if it is not the student's work, he or she will not be considered a viable applicant. Dr. Stone's clarity regarding the difference in guidance versus writing for the student gives much validity to this work.

In some ways, the writing of the college essay is a student's first act of true independence. By choosing the subject of the essay and putting their thoughts where strangers can read about their experiences, students are taking a risk, a leap of faith that the reader will hear their voice as it is meant to be heard. As mentors, the responsibility to guide but not lead, assist but not take over, take a step back and not step in too far, is like walking a tightrope. It is also an act of trust by the student and the family who has asked for a mentor's assistance and insight. By reading Dr. Stone's book, mentors will be prepared to walk the tightrope, guiding the student in a more profound way and creating a level of trust with the student that will lead to a strong, succinct, insightful essay—one that will help demonstrate that the student will fit in because the essay stands out!

I applaud Dr. Stone's work. While most students may not be admitted to every school to which they apply, mentors who use this resource should feel confident that their student had a strong essay as a foundation for the other components of the college application. I am honored to be given the opportunity to write this foreword, and I wish Dr. Stone, and all mentors, great success in the coming admission cycle.

Douglas L. Christiansen, Ph.D.
Vice Provost for Enrollment and Dean of Admissions
Associate Professor of Public Policy and Higher Education
Vanderbilt University

THE BETTER COLLEGE ESSAY

CHAPTER 1

INTRODUCTION

Parents, teachers, counselors, and others we'll call "mentors" can use this book and its tips to get the "Better Essay" from students—to probe and prod the student to dig deeply and think broadly and considerately as they tackle those college essays.

This book is about the "better" essay. Volumes have already been written about the "best" essay. For the purposes of this book, the goal is helping a student gain admission to a great college that they want to attend—be it competitive or less selective—and to write the best application essay the student can achieve.

In season three of the award-winning comedy *Modern Family*, Haley Dunphy has to write her college essay. Frustrated by her upper-middle class life of privilege, beautiful home in Southern California, good health, beauty, and loving parents, Haley blames her mother, Claire, for not providing her with fodder for an essay about overcoming adversity. Frustrated, Claire tricks Haley into the car for a drive in the mountains, dumps her on the side of the road, and leaves her there to find her way home without a cell phone or any money. Claire believed this would give Haley the "stuff" with which to write a winning college essay. Too bad Claire didn't have this book to guide Haley toward a Better Essay. She could have used this opportunity to have a conversation with Haley—to sit down and take stock of Haley's teenage years and help her develop an essay that was original and authentic. Claire would have learned a lot more about Haley, and perhaps Haley would have learned more about herself. Ultimately, Haley would have gotten into the college of her choice. In the television show, Haley didn't initially receive a single letter of admission. In the end, after being wait-listed, Haley briefly attended a college but was thrown out for poor conduct.

In the real world, Haley's angst over the essay, the ensuing battle with her mother, and the heightened tension in the household are actually a fairly accurate portrayal of what a lot of families experience when they enter the world of college admission. Hopefully, most parents don't turn to extreme measures such as dropping their child off in the wilderness just to make a point. Nonetheless, parents and students remain hopelessly confused about what the essay is all about, and parents feel helpless in guiding their student. Without guidance from a trained mentor, counselor, teacher, or parent, the student may work hours on an essay that "misses the point," is full of clichés they think a college wants to hear, or simply is not very interesting. There is a better way.

What is the college essay and why is it so important?

The number of students graduating from public high school in this country has never been higher. The National Center for Education Statistics estimated that 81 percent of students across the country in 2012 earned a diploma within four years of starting high school—the highest percentage of high school graduates in the past forty years. The biggest gains in high school graduation rates were among Hispanic and African-American students. More students are college-eligible, and the availability of financial aid for low-income families, along with aggressive programs to attract first-generation college students and international students, has made college accessible for hundreds of thousands more students than ever before.

Professor Jerome Karabel, who has studied the history of college admission since the establishment of the Ivy League colleges, writes that the shifts in admission to elite colleges from the children of alumni or graduates of feeder schools, to a system based more on merit, means that everyone has to demonstrate a high level of academic accomplishment for entry into the most selective schools. No one can bank on admission to an elite college. The shift to merit-based access has meant that all students, "even the children of the old upper class faced the prospect of rejection. The specter of downward mobility now extended to the most privileged section of the old elite—a development that would enduringly transform the atmosphere of the Big Three (Harvard, Yale, and Princeton)."

With increased competition for spots, colleges have used numerous devices to choose from the plethora of students clamoring to get in. The current list of colleges who are members of the Common Application exceeds 500 and they all share a single application portal. The Common Application requires students to write an essay based on one of five prompts. Other colleges, both private and public, that do not use the Common Application may ask for two essays equaling a minimum of 750 words—the University of California, for example—or offer an array of long and short essay choices. Common Application colleges often ask for "supplement" essays that can range from 150 to 1,000 words. The general essays usually offer broad topic choices, while the supplement essays often focus on the student explaining more specifically how they are a good fit for that particular college or specialized program, allowing the member colleges to obtain additional information that specifically addresses a student's interest in the college.

The essay is important for several reasons.

Admission standards vary by institution, but most colleges require a student transcript that shows the courses the student has taken, the rigor of those courses, and the grades received. Most colleges also require a standardized college entrance exam (the SAT or the ACT). Some also include the SAT Subject Tests and accept additional scores from International Baccalaureate exams or Advanced Placement exams. And while some colleges have gone "test optional," believing that the numerous biases of standardized tests and their lack of long-term predictive validity provide little guidance to admission officers in choosing the right students for the institution, most colleges include an essay component.

While still offered at some colleges, personal interviews have become a minor part of the application process due to the sheer volume of applicants. Because so few students are able to travel to interview, and the resources at the colleges can't handle thousands of individual meetings, the college essay serves to replace the intimacy that comes from having a face-to-face conversation with a student. The essay, therefore, allows the student to transcend the bucket of data offered to the college and to give the college an opportunity to gain a better understanding of the student—to know the student's interests and passions, to learn more about why the student has chosen their college, and to have some sense of the academic ability of the student which can be revealed through the writing process itself—the vocabulary, structure, and intellect of the student.

Colleges use student essays to make inferences about students. Because colleges have to make assumptions about which students will thrive on their campus and make their alma mater proud, the essay is a way for colleges to infer the personality of the students they seek to admit.

I asked Sam Gosling, a professor in the University of Texas at Austin's Department of Psychology and author of the best-selling book *Snoop: What Your Stuff Says About You*, if he felt that the inferences colleges make about students from their essays may not always be valid. "In the absence of direct experience, inferences or stereotypes fill in the gap when we are unable to gather all information," he said, adding that stereotypes and inferences allow people to make sense of the world when they are presented with only bits of information. Because colleges can't see you in all contexts, they do their best to fill these gaps with essays and other subjective material.

The effortlessness of applying online and the demise of the paper application have simplified the college admission process so that students can apply to multiple colleges with relative ease. Coupled with the competition to get into college, students are caught in a catch-22. More students applying to more colleges brings admission acceptance rates down lower and lower, so students panic and keep sending in more applications. It is no longer uncommon for students to apply to more than fifteen colleges. How, then, does a college know which of those schools a student really wants to attend? There really is no system that allows students to prioritize their interest and commitment, with the exception of binding Early Decision or Single Choice Restrictive Early Action plans.

This is where both fitting in and standing out enter the picture.

The college essay reminds me of a book I bought when I was pregnant. It had a list of baby names that assured the parents their moniker of choice would both "fit in and stand out." What exactly did that mean? The book listed names that were distinctive yet not so unusual or unpronounceable that your child would forever hate you. Fitting in and standing out is the goal of the college essay. The essay must stand out among thousands to admission officers. It must be original, insightful, and tell a new story they have not heard hundreds of times before. It needs to be clearly written, given an admission officer may only have a few minutes to read an entire essay. But the essay also must tell the college that this student will "fit"—that the student's ambitions and academic strengths will be a good match for the college. Haley Dunphy, as it turned out, wasn't a good fit, and who knows whether a Better Essay would have helped the college predict her success. For the sake of faith in the fairness of college admissions, this book will outline the process for adults to be collaborators with students, guiding them to writing the very best essay they can—one that will stand out, fit in, and ultimately lead the student to a successful college experience.

CHAPTER 2

THE LONG AND SHORT OF DYNAMIC ESSAYS: STANDING OUT

Essays come in a variety of forms: main essays (usually 500 to 700 words), supplemental essays of 200 to 300 words (sometimes counted as character counts, with or without spaces), and essays that allow for an elaboration of an activity or special circumstance for which there is no other place in the application to explain. Some supplemental essays, however, can be as long as 1,000 words. College essays, along with a detailed application form for listing demographic information, activities, work experience, high school courses, and honors and awards, make up the body of the application. Schools that use the Common Application and certain other colleges and universities also ask for letters of recommendations from teachers, counselors, and someone who knows the student well outside of school such as a member of the clergy, coach, employer, or youth group leader.

In this book, we'll discuss two main essay styles:

DYNAMIC: the "story or narrative." It is an essay that describes action and change. Students often refer to the college essay as a "personal statement." I like to steer students away from thinking of their essay as a statement. A dynamic essay is actually the converse of a statement because it allows the reader to follow the writer through a process of discovery.

CATEGORICAL: the essays that respond to questions requiring opinions and facts. These essays might be research-based; for example, essays that focus on objects, things, and categories. They also benefit from mentorship to come up with an interesting and original idea that adds the student's point of view and personality into what otherwise might be purely fact-based.

Here is an example of a DYNAMIC essay:

"If I were ten pounds of Gruyère cheese, what would be the fastest way to grate me?" I repeated this thought to myself over and over the night before I was to cater a brunch for 150 people who would be particularly upset if their bite of quiche was not cheesy enough. I had dealt with this kind of problem previously; after all, my friends and I had started our company, Three Friends Catering, over a year before. We knew how to get things done efficiently and how to work together to pull off an event seemingly effortlessly while reveling in the fact that we had slaved away for hours making perfect salmon mousse and filling it into that obnoxiously small hole in a cucumber slice with no one the wiser. But this was different. That night I was frantic, and the cheese line was a cry for help, as if I was asking the stuff to grate itself. My staff had cancelled on me at the last minute, and I was forced to rely on my mother and my sister to help me prepare the dozen quiches, twenty pounds of fruit salad, five huge bowls of green salad, and sixteen loaves of cranberry buckle bread. Then, at around 5:00 p.m., the phone rang. My mom was on the other end explaining how incredibly sorry she was that she and my sister had missed their flight out of Los Angeles and wouldn't be there to help me make the food. Suddenly, I was in charge of cooking brunch for 150 all by myself. I remember redirecting and refocusing my tactics. I made timelines of what needed to be done and I was prepared to work through the night to complete everything in time. I went into hyper-drive. I would not let anyone down—not my client, and especially not myself. I was up for the challenge and I wanted to do it alone. No one knew what to do as well as I did, and it was too late to call my friends. No, I knew that I needed to finish this myself. So, I forged on . . .

The dynamic college essay requires a student to turn inward—to relinquish a formula and evaluate his or her own experience in the first person. In high school English and history courses, most students learn to take a piece of literature or historical research and follow a fairly structured format to craft a response. These responses usually comply with a teacher's rubric and may be personal or written to defend a thesis or analyze a problem. The school essays are usually quite formal, follow a formula such as the five-paragraph essay, and are written in the third person. The college essay, however, presents a different challenge because the "grading" rubric is less clear. The evaluation process doesn't end with a grade or graduation, but with a more decisive response of a "Yes" or "No" letter from an admission office. The essays must "stand out" in their authenticity and originality.

Here are two examples of CATEGORICAL essays:

{ ESSAY 1 }

When I was fifteen, my mother, a freelance journalist, began writing an article about Mimi Silbert, a woman who is widely considered a "hero of the twenty-first century." She is the founder and CEO of the Delancey Street Foundation, a rehabilitation program for ex-convicts where the ex-convicts live together in dorms for four years and learn three trades before they "graduate" and live on their own. One evening, I had the privilege of having dinner with Ms. Silbert in her private dining room at the organization's restaurant while my mother interviewed her. Ms. Silbert's journey to success reminded me of my favorite passage from Alice in Wonderland, that the Queen would believe in at least six impossible things before breakfast. Ms. Silbert believed in an idea that every other criminologist in the world believed to be impossible-that the lowest and most violent criminals could be taught to live in normal society. The entire premise of her program was based solely on a gut feeling that every person on earth contained goodness. She believed that in order to access that goodness, one only needed to teach people that it existed inside of them. Her belief in the impossible and her bravery to question the current structure of our prison systems, work with dangerous people, and accept that she and the ex-convicts may, in fact, all fail together, allowed her to create the "most successful rehabilitation program in the world" as deemed by the California State Legislature. As a result, she has freed thousands of people from a life filled with crime, helplessness, and self-pity. I look at the world now with hope. That evening taught me that I must never lose faith in the goodness of people, regardless of whether or not I can see it. I can never stop believing in the impossible. Before I left, Ms. Silbert hugged me and told me that greatness can never occur if people like me are not willing to take a risk. It is not enough for me to believe in impossible things. I must also make them real.

{ ESSAY 2 }

The person who I would want to invite to the speaker's series is Supreme Court Justice Anthony McLeod Kennedy. My dad clerked for Justice Kennedy when he was on the 9th Circuit Court of Appeals. When I was young, I met him at a clerks' reunion. Now that I am older, I think I would better appreciate what he has to say. Kennedy is often the "swing vote" of the Supreme Court. He has been the tie-breaker on numerous 5-4 cases such as the recent Patient Protection and Affordable Care Act (Obamacare). I would like to hear Kennedy speak because I feel that he exemplifies many values that I find necessary for all good leaders to have, including a committment to service and equal rights for all.

Within the Categorical essay are two sub-categories:

FITTING IN: an essay that makes the argument about why the college is a good fit for the student.

ELABORATIVE: an essay that serves to explain or elaborate on other parts of the application (such as suspensions, special education needs, and work experiences). This type of essay will be discussed in more detail in Chapter 9.

Here is an example of a FITTING IN essay:

I knew that BU was the school for me when I spent two weeks this summer at the Summer Challenge Program. Taking Abnormal Psychology and Law, and also living in Warren Towers, I knew that this academic experience is what I wanted for the next four years. I visited again in October and after going on a tour, listening to an information session and speaking with Patrick McNally, I knew that Early Decision was what I wanted to do.

The College of Communication is where I want to be studying. I am a perfect fit for the Journalism major because I love to write, meet people, ask questions, do research, and travel. The Crisis Reporting Program specifically intrigues me because it involves the world and global health which are my current areas of interest. I am also fascinated by the New England Center for Investigative Reporting because my favorite part of journalism is the investigative and detective work. I would be so happy to combine my love for journalism with my passion for community service. It would be incredible to engage with the Boston community through work experience and service.

Lastly, imagining myself as part of the excitement and school spirit at a BU hockey game seals the deal. Boston University has everything I am looking for in a college and there is no other school I would want to attend.

. . . . ✳ . . . .

Here are two examples of ELABORATIVE essays:

I was diagnosed with a learning difference the beginning of junior year by an educational specialist. There is no specific name for my learning difference, but it does cause me to process slower than average. I am successful in school with extended time on tests and the use of a calculator on all math tests. I believe my grades improved after I started receiving extra test time. In addition, I have had some tutoring to learn strategies and study techniques to help me succeed.

In the following essay, a student named Serena discusses her work as a yearbook photographer. Rather than listing her accomplishments, she uses the essay to explain her artistic process—a process that requires her to think about not only her relationship to her art, but how her art affects her subjects. The essay takes the reader inward into the thought process of the photographer and what she values most about her work.

I am a photographer and I tell my stories one snapshot at a time. I look at everyday life and find the best way to visually represent the candid, uncut, and natural beauty of that moment. My goal is to create images that will resonate with my viewers and send a message. I have poured three years into being the head photographer for my high school's yearbook. I make an effort to build a relationship with each of my subjects and carry that mindset into each of my photos. I meet my subjects in two ways, as their friend and their witness. As a friend, I strive to understand exactly what their emotions are. As a witness, I articulate how I want them to be seen in their element. I do the research necessary to understand them and to tell the story that they want told through my lens. I take photos of people at eye level because I like to build a balanced relationship that doesn't leave anyone inferior or too empowered.

With the students I counsel, it seems that writing the college essay is often the first time, perhaps since early in elementary school, that the student has been asked to be introspective, and where there isn't a right or wrong answer. Students worry both about seeming boastful and not appearing confident enough. They aren't sure who their audience is or what exactly the college will take away from the essay. "Is it too personal? Do I sound too rich or entitled? Do I sound whiney or compulsive? If I say I work very hard at academics, will they think I'm not smart? Or if I write that high school was easy, will they think I wasn't challenged—or even worse, lazy?"

The word count is limited, and instead of being given a teacher's feedback, which might allow for revision, the college essay comes with no feedback. A student's essay will be evaluated for college entrance, but the student perceives the reader as anonymous and therefore is insecure about how it will be received. If you write a letter to your best friend, you can be fairly certain she'll understand your humor or that she'll read into a story the background of the writer. This is not the case when writing for someone who doesn't know you. There is no filling in the blanks of information left untold—no one will be able to tell if you are being serious or sarcastic. The essay has to stand on its own and leave no room for interpretation.

Audience

"It is clear to me when a student has sought advice about a college essay, and when they have let it go to be a last-minute draft. A mentor encourages her students to think critically about a topic, helping them to develop an essay that not only speaks to the students' strengths and aspirations, but an institution's own values. People joke that the college application essay is one of the most important essays that your student will ever write; and I'm here to say, it is no joke! It's very important that your student thinks deeply about a topic and writes an essay that provides insight into who they are, and what they're going to bring to a college community. I so appreciate the work mentors do for students; it makes the college applications process so much more enjoyable, be it for the student or admissions counselor!"
–University Admissions Counselor, North Carolina

Colleges vary in how they evaluate the college application. Some colleges will have two readers, and if the readers don't agree on an admit or deny, it goes to a third reader. At other colleges, particularly those with fewer resources, it may be a single individual who reads the application. Some applications are decided on "by committee" and a student's essay might appear in a boardroom on a PowerPoint for several members of the admission committee to review. It may be held up next to the student's writing section on the SAT or ACT to verify that the submitted college essay was written with little outside assistance and appears to be written by the same person who provided an essay sample on the college entrance exam.

The entrance exam essay differs from the application essay because the student is given a single prompt and limited time to respond. The SAT or ACT essay provides the college with a snapshot of a student's spontaneous writing—the grammar, syntax, and strength of his or her persuasive skills—but it is not a thoughtful, personal essay where the student has ample time to consider and formulate a response. And, as shall be explored further, it is not generally a dynamic story that provides insight into the student's identity.

When I ask students to imagine who will read their essay, they often think it's a grey-haired professorial type or an adult about the same age as their parents. In fact, most recruiters are often just a few years out of college and in their early twenties. Students will have an easier time knowing their audience if they make some personal connection to the college recruiter for this reason. They can contact the regional recruiter by phone, e-mail, or Skype, or meet that individual if he or she visits their high school or college fair. Knowing whom they are writing to will certainly make the task less formidable.

Types of Applications and Essays

There are many types of college applications for private and public colleges, for-profit colleges, and international universities. But the Common Application is shared by more than 500 colleges in the United States as well as by some non-U.S. schools, such as Saint Andrews in Scotland and Jacobs University in Bremen, Germany. The Common Application is a non-profit organization that requires member colleges to provide a holistic review of an application. This means that the colleges commit to reviewing the student's application beyond grades and test scores and evaluate the essay along with letters of recommendation. Schools that use the Common Application are mostly private colleges, but some public colleges use it as well. One of the student's first tasks should be to learn which colleges he or she is applying to use the Common Application.

The prompts for the Common Application introduced in 2013 require a minimum of 250 words and a maximum of 650 words. Prior to 2013, the word limit was 500 words.

Six-hundred-fifty words is about two and a half pages of text. Here are the instructions, the questions, and short examples that are excerpts from completed essays. People often refer to this part of the application as the Personal Statement, or simply "the long essay." We'll refer to these essay prompts, and others like them, as "dynamic."

INSTRUCTIONS

The essay demonstrates your ability to write clearly and concisely on a selected topic and helps you distinguish yourself in your own voice. What do you want the readers of your application to know about you apart from courses, grades, and test scores? Choose the option that best helps you answer that question and write an essay of no more than 650 words, using the prompt to inspire and structure your response. Remember: 650 words is your limit, not your goal. Use the full range if you need it, but don't feel obligated to do so. (The application won't accept a response shorter than 250 words.)

COMMON APPLICATION ESSAY QUESTIONS AND EXCERPTS OF STUDENT WORK WITH COMMENTARY

{ PROMPT 1 }

Some students have a background or story that is so central to their identity that they believe their application would be incomplete without it. If this sounds like you, then please share your story.

Whenever I walk into a Chinese restaurant with my family, we're one of the many Chinese-American families waiting to be seated among the cramped tables to eat pork buns or bowls of steaming congee. But when one of the waiters notices my family, he or she inevitably asks us, "Ji wei?" No matter how many times my family of four is asked this simple question, our response is always the same: we stare blankly at the waiter before holding up four fingers.

One might think that, as an Asian kid growing up in the Bay Area (where nearly every fourth person is of Asian descent), I would fit in perfectly fine; however, living in California means I'm surrounded every day by first-generation Chinese-Americans who may superficially resemble me but are otherwise vastly different.

In this essay, Winston touches on the stereotypes he feels it necessary to dispel. He knows that the reader will see he is of Asian-American heritage, and he uses the essay as an opportunity to counter assumptions people might make about him. At the same time, his story about identity is central to experiences in high school and in his hometown.

. . . .   ✳   . . . .

{ PROMPT 2: }

Recount an incident or time when you experienced failure. How did it affect you, and what lessons did you learn?

———————

The greatest failure I have ever experienced was when I did not get first chair in my school orchestra. Later, I realized that my failure was really only a disappointment and I was able to come out of the situation stronger. In my orchestra, the first chairs are student leaders who help manage their musical section. It is an honor to be a first chair because of the caliber of our orchestra, which earned unanimous superiors last year at the Musical Education Association competition.

In my section, violin, there is one student who sits in the first chair who has responsibilities such as taking attendance, relaying messages from the conductor, and passing out new music. I wanted to be chosen as first chair to show how much passion I had for the orchestra and to be a role model for the other musicians.

I appreciate this student's honesty about the jealousy and competition she felt toward her classmates. Acknowledging that other students shared similar goals was a big step for this student. It's easy to boast about your triumphs, but much more humbling to discuss disappointments.

{ PROMPT 3: }

Reflect on a time when you challenged a belief or idea. What prompted you to act? Would you make the same decision again?

———————————

"Don't cry, Alice," I said to myself as I gripped my pen tightly and scribbled on my notebook. Larry sat across from me on his musky leather couch, grabbing tissues to wipe the tears falling down from his face as he remembered the fateful night of November 4, 2008, the night that California passed Proposition 8, the ballot measure that illegalized same-sex marriages and possibly nullified existing marriages between same-sex couples, like that of Larry and his husband. I kept willing myself not to cry, trying to remain a completely professional journalist, but I felt a few tears forming in my eyes. I smiled as I thought about how strange this situation was: here I was, crying with a fifty-year-old man whom I had just met five minutes ago. I had come to interview Larry and his family for my story in the school newsmagazine on Proposition 8 and its effects on the gay- and lesbian-headed households at my school. I had read many newspaper articles about Proposition 8 and the groups working either for or against it, but none of the stories I had read had detailed the psychological effects on the families and the children of these gay and lesbian couples who were caught in the middle of a huge political battle. My yearning to dig deeper than the politics of the issue and discover how these people felt led me to Larry's living room.

Alice's first draft of this essay was categorical. She wrote about the issues with the legislation and its impact on gay couples from a strictly journalistic position. In her second draft, a dynamic story, she takes the same political position but uses this essay to describe what it *felt* like to be a journalist. She intentionally strays from her role as a reporter and allows her own emotions to come through. The essay tells us that Alice is a sensitive person, willing to write an unpopular viewpoint because she believes that the "other" side of the story needs to be told.

{ PROMPT 4: }

Describe a place or environment where you are perfectly content. What do you do or experience there, and why is it meaningful to you?

———————————

My alarm blares at 4:00 a.m. every Thursday morning.

I roll myself out of bed, fortified by the knowledge that I'm not the only one getting up at this absurd hour. Sleepy and grumpy, I pull on my rowing gear, wolf down some cereal, grab my backpack and head out.

I do enjoy the quiet of the predawn chill and darkness. By 5:00 a.m., I'm at the Brittingham Boathouse on Monona Bay in Madison. As more rowers arrive, the chatter picks up and I start to feel excited about getting onto the water.

I'm truly content after a satisfying workout with my team.

This is a great example of describing a place of contentment while weaving in details about a significant activity in the student's résumé. In this essay, the student was able to identify where he is content while also describing quite eloquently the moment an athlete finds contentment with himself as part of a team.

{ PROMPT 5: }

Discuss an accomplishment or event, formal or informal, that marked your transition from childhood to adulthood within your culture, community, or family.

———————————

I was waiting for a young woman, Linda, to come out of the shower at the Coalition for Homeless Youth where I volunteer every week. I sat in my usual metal chair outside of the shower room. The clipboard with the list of names of the people lined up for the shower rested on my lap, along with the timer. When the timer went off, I knocked on the door for Linda to come out. Linda walked out of the shower wearing a colorful skirt, slightly torn at the hem, and a white blouse. I was confused because I wasn't used to seeing someone come out of the shower in clean clothes. She was smiling as she was putting on a little make up so I asked her what was the occasion. She told me that today was her wedding day. I was so surprised and amazed that someone from the homeless population of Chicago was going to be married.

This student chose to use her increasing responsibilities as a volunteer in a community organization to demonstrate her transition to an adult role within that organization. This essay elaborates on an important extracurricular activity while simultaneously showing how the student's thinking shifted to a more mature understanding of homelessness.

The final drafts of these excerpts are shown in Chapter 10.

Supplement Essays

Many colleges that use the Common Application require students to write Supplement Essays. Supplements are additional essays that generally range from 150 to 750 words, though they are sometimes counted in characters (with or without spaces), with prompts created by the individual colleges. Colleges that use their own applications, rather than the Common Application, may also ask for short essays in addition to a longer essay.

Colleges use supplement essays for various purposes. A college may add additional questions to prevent a student from randomly submitting applications to colleges in which they have little interest because there is no additional work to be done by the student. Requiring a supplement lets the college know that the student didn't just hit another "submit" button, but actually put some thought into selecting that particular college. The "common" aspect of the application makes it simple for a student to send off potentially dozens of applications with little more than some additional application fees. The supplements are also a tool for a college to ask a student to respond to questions where the "fit" is investigated. The college wants to see how a student tackles an intellectual question or how he or she will contribute directly to the campus community. The supplements also allow the college to ask questions that specifically address the school's mission and values. Chapter 6 will explore more about "fit." The examples below demonstrate the variety of questions that can be asked of students in this section of the application.

Here are some examples of supplement essay prompts, in which the best responses vary between dynamic writing and categorical writing.

{ AMHERST COLLEGE }

(Students can choose one prompt to respond to out of several.)
It is not necessary to research, read, or refer to the texts from which these quotations are taken; we are looking for original, personal responses to these short excerpts. Remember that your essay should be personal in nature and not simply an argumentative essay.

"Literature is the best way to overcome death. My father, as I said, is an actor. He's the happiest man on earth when he's performing, but when the show is over, he's sad and troubled. I wish he could live in the eternal present, because in the theater, everything remains in memories and photographs. Literature, on the other hand, allows you to live in the present and to remain in the pantheon of the future. Literature is a way to say, I was here, this is what I thought, this is what I perceived. This is my signature, this is my name."–Ilan Stavans, Professor of Spanish, Amherst College, from "The Writer in Exile: an interview with Ilan Stavans" by Saideh Pakravan for the fall 1993 issue of *The Literary Review*

Length: 300 words maximum

{ CLAREMONT-MCKENNA COLLEGE (CMC) }

Leadership is a constant theme and emphasis at CMC. One way CMC emphasizes leadership is through the Athenaeum Speaker Series (www.cmc.edu/mmca), which enables CMC students to dine with leaders from a wide range of fields every weeknight during the academic year. Recent speakers have included authors, activists, entrepreneurs, scientists, professors, politicians, and more.

If you could invite anyone to speak at the Athenaeum, who would you choose and why?

Length: Recommend more than a sentence, less than a page.

······························ ✳ ······························

{ STANFORD UNIVERSITY }

(Students respond to all three supplement questions.)
Stanford students possess an intellectual vitality. Reflect on an idea or experience that has been important to your intellectual development.

Length: 2,000 characters maximum

Virtually all of Stanford's undergraduates live on campus. Write a note to your future roommate that reveals something about you or that will help your roommate—and us—know you better.

Length: 2,000 characters maximum

What matters to you, and why?

Length: 2,000 characters maximum

Supplement questions range from very straight-forward (why a student is interested in a particular major) to very complex (comment on a famous alumni's words from the 1800s). Students often leave supplements to the last minute, as they spend so much time with the main college essay. The supplements require an equal level of commitment and should be reviewed with the student early on in the process.

······························ ✳ ······························

{ THE UNIVERSAL COLLEGE APPLICATION }

Fewer than fifty colleges use the Universal Common Application. This application allows students to write on any topic in under 500 words and upload a link that provides the college with personal information, such as a visual arts portfolio or dance supplement. Several colleges use both the Universal College Application and the Common Application, allowing students to choose which system to use. These schools include Yale, Harvard, Princeton, and the University of Chicago.

{ UNIQUE COLLEGE APPLICATIONS }

Many colleges prefer the use of an application that is under their own control, allowing them to choose their own set of questions for students' responses. Some questions that have appeared in applications specific to singular colleges include these examples used for the past several years by the University of California.

············· ✳ ·············

{ UNIVERSITY OF CALIFORNIA }

250 words minimum per question; Questions 1 & 2 combined must be a maximum 1,000 words

---

1. Describe the world you come from—for example, your family, community, or school—and tell us how your world has shaped your dreams and aspirations.

2. Tell us about a personal quality, talent, accomplishment, contribution or experience that is important to you. What about this quality or accomplishment makes you proud, and how does it relate to the person you are?

Some college essays also enter students into merit competitions for either scholarships or Honors College placement. Elon University in North Carolina, for example, uses a unique application that doubles as a competition for an award of up to $5,000. This is where it's clear how important the essay is, not only for admission but also for accolades that can be earned along with admission.

············· ✳ ·············

{ ELON UNIVERSITY }

Here are the essay questions posed by Elon University in 2014. Applicants had to answer one of three prompts in approximately 500 words:

---

1. Imagine you are traveling to a new country. While you are there you meet members of the local community. As you engage in conversation with them you pull

three items out of your bag to tell them about you and your culture. What are these items and what is their significance?

2. Choose a literary character that experienced a great personal struggle or challenge. Briefly describe this challenge and how the character overcame it. Why did this have an impact on you? Are there ways in which you identify with this character?

3. If you were given $10,000 to invest in a project you are passionate about or a business you want to start, what would it be and why? Who would benefit and how would you spend the money? Be specific about the goals you hope to achieve.

If all of this seems confusing, that's because it is. With the increasing competition for college admission, it's not uncommon for students to apply to ten to fifteen colleges—and write numerous application essays.

Just keeping track of all the essay topics and the demands of each individual college can be an overwhelming task. Students can make a spreadsheet of the number of essays required and mark questions that "overlap" on a similar theme—then make an assessment of all the writing that must be accomplished and strategize the most efficient way to complete each application.

CHAPTER 3

THE PSYCHOLOGY OF THE ESSAY WRITER

What makes the difference between an essay a student can write alone and the Better Essay a student can write with a mentor? The answer lies deep in personality psychology research and the research areas of social cognition and personal conceptualization.

Consider that, if you were to ask a student to tell you about him or herself, you would initially get a long list of traits, such as kind, extroverted, ambitious, or friendly. Asking further questions might elicit another level of descriptiveness, such as where a person lives and his or her interests or skills, position in his or her family, affiliations (such as Muslim, Boy Scout, trumpet player, or soccer goalie), or perhaps even his or her goals or values—for example, "I'd like to run a business after college," or, "I love animals and hope to become a veterinarian."

Psychologists refer to the ability to describe the self or others as social cognition, and, specifically, person conceptualization. Person conceptualization is a developmental process, meaning children initially can't easily differentiate themselves from others, and as children develop, so do their social cognitive skills. Children's descriptions of themselves are egotistic and undifferentiating. In late adolescence, where our prospective college students are, they should have reached a higher level of social cognition, but not quite at the level of mature adults. Teens might be expected to be able to describe traits, behaviors, feelings, or reactions that are qualified, conditional, and modified using "but" or "although." They might be able to describe themselves with a trait (like "outgoing," for example) and modify it with a statement such as, "I'm very outgoing with my friends but it takes me quite a while to become comfortable in new situations and show my sense of humor."

Adults, on the other hand, typically can describe traits and behaviors psychologically. They can provide perspective on the roots of their experiences and what has influenced their experiences, and reflect on the origins of their traits or behaviors.

Dan McAdams, a professor at Northwestern University, studies what it takes to know a person beyond traits and descriptions. His work supports the notion that an insightful person can "steadily build an understanding of another person as they move from one stage of knowing to the next." The goal of the mentor in getting students to reveal authentic versions of themselves is to express their self as they develop over time and to define who they are . . . in other words, to reveal their identity. McAdams refers to this type of storytelling as "autobiographical reasoning."

In "The Power of Stories in Personality Psychology," Margarita Tartakovsky summarizes what we are looking for in the better college essay: "These stories become a process of 'integration' bringing together into an understandable frame disparate ideas, characters, happenings, and other elements of life that were previously set apart." As students try to find meaning in everything from a minor event to major life experiences, they are demonstrating "autobiographical reasoning."

There is a reason why celebrities choose to tell all to a skilled interviewer like Barbara Walters, Terry Gross, or Oprah Winfrey. These extraordinarily skilled interviewers can get the "story" out of these celebrities and even get them to reveal more than they may have intended. Celebrities could get enough publicity with their own tell-all, but the process of being interviewed, probed, and pushed certainly ups the ratings. In any case, we believe as viewers that we have seen the celebrity in a deeper, more genuine way.

McAdams's ultimate goal in the process of using an interviewer is this revelation of identity. According to Gosling, "Rarely is someone able to describe his or her identity on demand. It needs to be drawn out." McAdams believes that identities are revealed through the telling of the story. His interview process is not developed to help students write the college essay, nor do most counselors have the time to develop long relationships. But there are techniques that mentors can use to get at the story quickly in order to help students respond to a college application essay prompt.

A dynamic essay truly becomes a Better Essay when the student can, in the essay itself, reveal this cognitive shift. When a student has the "aha" moment of understanding a situation in a new way and can carry the reader through that thought process, an essay really stands out.

Professor Peter Lapote, an essayist and professor at Columbia University, wrote a New York Times piece on his experience helping his daughter with her college essay. As an essayist, he described the Better Essay, the responsibility of the mentor to push the student to write of her inner debate, and his frustration with the student's English teacher, who thought the essay should be a classic position paper.

"Argumentation is a good skill to have, but the real argument should be with oneself," said Lapote. "Especially when it comes to the development of young writers, it is crucial to nudge them past that self-righteous inveighing, that shrill, defensive one-track that is deadly for personal essays or memoirs, and encourage a more polyphonic, playful approach. That may be why a classic essay technique is to stage an inner debate by thinking against oneself . . . "

In categorical essays, the student also needs to reveal his or her identity. This essay may focus on a factual issue, such as a political topic, how they will live with a roommate, or why a piece of art is significant. A student has to justify a position or an opinion in a categorical essay. It doesn't necessarily have to describe the development of a position, but the Better Essay will embed information into the essay that the college can use, as Gosling would say, "to snoop." The students need to be aware that the college really doesn't particularly care whether their interests and passions lie in toxic trash in India or which Supreme Court Justice is the better speech-maker. The college wants to know why students care about these issues, how it relates to their own identity, and what inspires their passion. They also want to see how well their opinions can be supported by relevant facts.

This is an example of a categorical essay that reveals much about the student:

Describe a creative work (as in art, music, science, writing, etc.) that has had an influence on you, and explain that influence.

It was spring of sophomore year, nearly halfway through my high school experience, and it seemed like everyone but me had their futures all planned out. Then we read The Great Gatsby, *and everything became clear. I was captivated by the juxtaposition of Nick Carraway and Jay Gatsby, and I soon discovered that they represented the two ways of life that I was grappling with at the moment. It comes down to the conflict between being the "specialist" or the "well-rounded man." I envied my classmates—the star soccer player, the class president, the amazing vocalist, because they were the very best at the single activity they practiced, and like Gatsby, they received the appropriate recognition. I, on the other hand, saw myself in the same boat as Nick: a dabbler and observer with bits of experience in multiple different fields. However, one look at Gatsby's fate had me reconsidering the prudence of devoting all one's time to a single dream. Gatsby's single-sighted pursuit of Daisy blinded him to the impracticability of his fantasy and prevented him from seeing everything else his life had to offer; he died lonely and unsatisfied. Perhaps Mr. Carraway had it right after all. Rather than attach himself to one ambition, he let his curiosity guide him in a myriad of directions. The only way to experience life fully is to constantly experiment, Gatsby taught me.*

In this essay, the student, responding to a piece of literature and its influence on her, compares her own values to that of two major characters in the book. Yael describes her own predicament as she observes the successes of her classmates. She is concerned that her desire to be well-rounded might not be valued by others in her community, nor by the colleges to which she is applying. Using a piece of literature as a springboard, Yael allows the colleges to better understand her choice to engage in many activities throughout high school, and how her understanding of the characters in Gatsby gives her confidence to live her life as she chooses.

CHAPTER 4

THE GOALS AND GROUND RULES: THE COLLABORATIVE PROCESS

The questions on the college essay usually seem quite intimidating even to an adult—so it often seems like an insurmountable task to adolescents, even overwhelmingly so, because the they haven't developed the social cognitive skills to tackle them. But the mentor can help the student break down the questions and generate creative responses.

Greatness often comes with collaboration and partnership, the solicitation of feedback, and working with someone who pushes your perceived limits. Steve Jobs had Steve Wozniak. They brought different skills to the task and created products beyond what either of them may have achieved if they had believed they had to go it alone. It's okay for adults to be that mentor in the college application process.

Supreme Court Justice Sandra Sotomayor said in a radio interview with San Francisco's Michael Krasny that every student is better with a mentor. Raised in a poor neighborhood in the South Bronx, Sotomayor credits her academic and professional success to finding mentors along the way. On the speaking circuit for her book, *My Beloved World*, she advised students who are writing an essay to get someone to read it and get feedback before the final draft is turned in. And if the first person you ask isn't helpful, she said, keep asking. Keep working until you get it right. Sotomayor believes, as do I, that it is the collaboration between two minds that brings out the best in a student.

I love the quote from Lake Wobegon, "Where all the children are above average." Wouldn't we love that to be true? But all students, no matter what their academic record might indicate, can write a Better Essay with a mentor who can help a student discover what is interesting to write about or what is unique, and then provide constructive feedback. A B student shouldn't be expected to write what an English teacher would consider an A+ essay—that's not a realistic expectation, and in fact, an A+ essay from a student who didn't pass the AP English exam would look suspect. But a compelling essay, I believe, can be written by anyone—and some of the essays I have found most memorable, most poignant, and most original haven't necessarily come from the most academically gifted students. But I think they brought a lot of heart and honesty to the task, and that's what made those essays stick with me.

To this end, there is both a goal and a process to reach that goal. So before you begin working with the student you will mentor, think about what the goals are.

The Goals for the Mentor

Above all else, the mentor needs to be a listener and someone that the student believes is trustworthy and non-judgmental, while at the same time providing honest and constructive feedback. If the student is not your child confidentiality must be guaranteed. There are many days when I feel more like a psychotherapist than an educational consultant because, in the process of finding the story, a lot of very personal information comes to the surface. I may be the first person outside the family with whom a student discusses coming out as gay. I may become part of a small circle of adults who know of a student's rape or a family member's suicide. A student's story may reveal abuse, an eating disorder, or a terrible relationship with a parent. These conversations don't always end up being the focus of an essay, but much will be shared in the process of helping an adolescent find their story. The mentor must establish trust, and the best way to do this is by meeting with the student alone.

Often, a parent is intent on being part of the essay process. But this isn't the parent's essay. To establish trust with the student, and to elicit the authentic essays which are the goal, the student needs the privacy and space to explore many topics without worrying what the reaction of the parent will be. If it's the parent who is mentoring the student, trust can be established by working with the student in a private space—away from the other parent, siblings, or anyone else who could overhear. For non-parent mentors, a comfortable room, office, or coffee shop will do. I work by Skype with students too far to come to one of my offices. Skype fills the screen with the student's face, so even though there is a geographic distance between the student and me, the space feels very personal and private.

The first formal step in being a mentor to a student is to make a pact. The pact is a written agreement between student and mentor that designates the mentor as the only one who works with the student on the essay. I let students show their essays to others and elicit verbal comments, but the student must bring them to me before the ideas are either incorporated into the paper or discarded. A commitment to have one mentor is essential for the work to progress. Too many opinions and too many edit marks will result in an essay that has lost the student's voice and, just as important, will no longer be owned by the student. Sometimes students are a little bit unprepared to make that commitment to a mentor, but the commitment is essential, so the first place to start is to come to an agreement. In can be formal or informal, but sitting down with the student and going over the expectations of both writer and mentor is a necessary step. In my work, the parent signs the contract as well. Here is my contract:

I will be the primary person working with you on your essays and applications. You agree not to let teachers, parents, or other individuals edit your work. As part of my process, I have "secret" readers take a look at your essays to provide me with additional feedback, which I will share with you. You are welcome to get feedback as well, but not to make any changes or alterations without reviewing the feedback with me. There are many ways/styles to approach essay writing—working with a single individual ensures that your essay is authentic to your writing style and ideas.

The Goals for the Student

The goals for the student are to create essays that are authentic. Authenticity means that the essay reflects the true experiences and point of view of the writer. They aren't fabricated to impress. They impress because of their authenticity.

Students should create essays that are original. Teenagers do share common experiences, whether it is encountering poverty for the first time on a service-learning trip, being left on the bench by a coach, being teased about weight, having trouble with divorced parents, or simply feeling like they don't fit in. These aren't topics that need to be avoided, but they are themes that need a twist so they sound personal and don't make the student look like the thousands of other teens who have had similar "life-changing" experiences. Approached from a fresh and creative perspective, these topics can make for truly original essays.

It is not a requirement of the writer to "tell all." There are some things better left unsaid. The college application essay is not an application for psychotherapy. The number of first draft essays I've seen where the student writes about their obsessions, their profound anxiety, or their depression would scare an admission officer. I once saw a student who was re-applying to colleges after being denied admission at every single college he had applied to after high school. He ended up taking a gap year and trying again. He showed me the essay he had used in the prior round, which started with, "I have had a terrible history of angry and violent outbursts." One of the colleges he had applied to that prior year contacted him and told him that, given what he had written in his application essay, they were not going to admit him. Personal problems can be explained in more subtle terms.

The student is responsible for developing, to the best of his or her ability, a grammatically correct and a well-written essay that is consistent with the academic work the student will also be submitting. This means students shouldn't expect their mentors to spell-check their work—that should be easy enough for a student to do even if she or he isn't a great speller. A college isn't expecting a student who scores in the high 400s on the SAT critical reading or writing sections to demonstrate a wide breadth of vocabulary and sentence structure. But a rambling essay without structure makes the student who scored in the top 20 percent on the SAT look un-invested. Colleges often compare the written portion of the SAT to the college essay the student submits. They will expect a more fully formed thesis on the college essay, but they also expect to sense it was written by the same writer. Thus, the college essay must look like there's been some investment in time and effort.

Students should be prepared to fully answer the question being asked. That doesn't mean there isn't room for a bit of interpretation, but ignoring the question and answering without giving thought to the college's intent isn't going to impress.

Students should feel comfortable accepting constructive feedback and be brave enough to try ideas, discard what doesn't work, and write, re-write, and re-write again. It's not uncommon for the students I work with to write ten drafts of an essay. These aren't complete re-writes, but in the end, the students eventually become their own critics, working harder than ever to meet their goals.

I often have a difficult time convincing a parent to let me work alone with a student. Sometimes parents feel they need to sit in on an essay-writing meeting to give input or fill in details they feel the student might leave out, or perhaps the parents just want to feel like they have an important role in the process. The parent's role, if not that of mentor, is to allow the student to explore ideas independently. It's not necessary for a parent to fill in the blanks, because the essay isn't an extracurricular résumé where the omissions of dates or places or inaccuracies of memory will be problematic. The essay is the place for the exploration of personal ideas and thoughts. The student has to have the mental space to make that exploration with the mentor only.

The mentor has to establish boundaries. This is very important. If the mentor is not the parent, it has to be clearly determined with the parent, before the process begins, that the essay belongs to the student.

When I first started working with students to develop wonderful and insightful essays, I learned that a parent who insisted on reading and commenting on (or sometimes drastically changing) an essay could sabotage the whole process. I naïvely thought that the parents of a particular student—I'll call her Sally—would be proud of her work and that they would appreciate the thought and effort that went into it. Sally had written about her affluent community and her success in creating a neighborhood improvement project. Instead, Sally's parents accused me of helping the student write about them negatively, portraying them and their wealthy neighborhood as self-indulgent. This incident created tremendous stress and embarrassment for the student, and put me in the position of having to dissipate the tension among all of us so the student could continue her task of completing an authentic essay.

Now, before embarking on the process with the student, I recommend coming to an agreement with the parent or parents and student regarding access and control. Parental involvement is a sticky topic and one with which I still struggle. I believe that the essay is the property of the student—not the parent—just as much as a term paper or school report. But parents may feel too much is at stake with the college essay and want to control the outcome. Fortunately, many students and parents don't keep secrets. Most parents do trust their students and will trust their mentor. But if the trust isn't there, the mentor and student need to know if the parents have veto power. If they do, then the process can still proceed, but the student will have to tread more lightly and the mentor may need to advise the student to avoid topics that the parents might find too personal.

CHAPTER 5

THE MENTOR'S TOOLKIT

It's no surprise, given the difficulty of the prompts just reviewed, that both mentors and students sometimes just want to throw their hands up in their air and fall into despair. There is no doubt that these questions are challenging. To keep a student from becoming completely overwhelmed, a mentor can assist a student in reviewing all of the requirements for each school and then start with the most general essay. This would likely mean starting with the Common Application or the longest essay the student will need to write.

The process starts with the mentor's tools:

The student résumé (I have provided a template in the Appendix) is a list of all the student's academic and extracurricular activities, accomplishments, employment history, and volunteer work from the start of high school.

The résumé should:

- Be neatly organized

- Be chronological

- Be separated into major headings

- Be free of spelling errors

- Indicate dates and length of time in activities

- Be presentable to show an admission officer on request or give to a teacher who is writing a letter of recommendation

The **PARENT QUESTIONNAIRE** (see Appendix) is completed by one or both parents. The questionnaire covers basic demographic information and includes a few very helpful responses:

a) Pretend you are writing your student's letter of recommendation for college: What are your student's strengths? What are your student's weaknesses?

b) What are your goals for your student's college experience?

c) What do you and your student agree on and disagree on at home?

The **STUDENT QUESTIONNAIRE** (see Appendix) is completed by the student and asks:

a) What do you and your parents tend to agree on? Where do you disagree?

b) Have you traveled?

c) What activities do you enjoy now?

d) What activities do you hope to experience or try in college?

e) Has your education been disrupted at any time?

f) Have you ever visited a college campus? Where? When?

g) Do you know what a college major is? A minor? Have you considered what you might like to study in college?

The high school transcript, along with a list of senior year courses, should also be shared with the mentor to provide additional context.

Standardized Test Scores (ACT, SAT, AP)

The mentor can review all of this information before meeting with the student. The tools help the mentor understand where the student is academically, their overall knowledge of colleges and how they function, and how experienced the student may be in talking about college.

How to Approach an Essay

Intensive study of the résumé may begin to reveal how the student will "stand out," but there is more to a student than a list of accomplishments. The questionnaire can be helpful in providing greater context to the student's experiences. Nevertheless, this is a good place to start to get to know a student. With his or her résumé and questionnaire in hand, I begin the process of interviewing the student.

I ask students to come to our essay meeting without anything written, and I don't ask them to look at the prompts in advance. Initially, I just want to get to know the student better. Together, we go through the résumé and the parent and student questionnaires. I ask them about their level of participation in activities and the level of importance of different experiences. I also want to know if they attended a neighborhood high school or if they've had the experience of going through an application process to a private or specialized high school. This material provides a bit of a frame around the future story. This first meeting would typically take about an hour, but it could require a follow-up meeting, allowing the student some time to reflect on what we've talked about between each visit.

After reviewing the background information, we look at the Common Application prompts or the main essay prompts for non-Common App schools.

Together, the students and I review the long essay questions. I ask the students to read each one aloud to me. Reading aloud is often uncomfortable for students, but when they read aloud, I can tell whether they understand the question. Do they stumble over words? Where do they pause? Do they shake their head "no way"—or do they smile? We don't select a question to focus on just yet. But the prompts are now in front of us as we proceed to discover the student's narrative.

As we go through the questions, and the students provide ideas, I take notes. When I find an idea I like, that I think will be rich enough to write 650 words, I ask them to tell me the story. Students usually want to start with a chronology of events. It's okay for them to begin to organize a story chronologically, but it doesn't usually make for a very interesting essay. As we go through the chronology, I might make a notation of a starting place. It could be at the beginning, middle, or end, depending on where I think the story will go. I take notes while the students talk, write down phrases they have used, and sometimes record the conversations so that they can play them back to re-work the story.

I summarize the different ideas the student has and try to help him or her connect experiences. This is where the theory of McAdams comes into play. I am helping the students integrate their ideas. For example, I worked with a student who was a professional actor. Santiago was very small for his age, and while he was practicing for his driving test, he was still playing eight-year-old characters, such as Dill in the play *To Kill a Mockingbird*. We talked about all of the characters he had played, and a common theme that emerged was that he wore pajamas in every play. I asked him to describe the pajamas to me: they were plaid, they had feet sewn in, they were flannel, and one even came with bunny ears. He felt ridiculous one moment in the driver's seat of his parents' Toyota, navigating city highways, when later in the afternoon he'd take on the persona of a small child. He began to talk more about the pressure his agents put on him not to change his voice or grow any taller while in rehearsal for his next big production. But, of course, he had no control over those events. Over three meetings, we talked about what happened when his voice did change and he could no longer be a child star. We talked about what it would be like to play age-appropriate characters, and how his sense of self would change along with the costumes he would be wearing. He was able to write a terrific essay that took the reader through the shift in his thought process, from initial terror at the end of playing child roles, to his growing comfort with acting parts commensurate with his age. In the end, he was able to explain his identity as an actor and integrate these separate experiences into an overarching essay about his physical and emotional maturation.

A tag was safety pinned to the back of the pajamas. It read: "Memorial Theatre Costume Shop. Actor: Santiago Torres. Role: Buddy. Production: A Christmas Memory." The familiar smell of backstage dust lingered on the baby blue striped pajamas I was wearing. I played a young Truman Capote whose antics with his elderly cousin got him into trouble. I used to complain about the streak of consecutive shows in which I had to wear pajamas, considering the fact that I was older than all the characters I played, but the truth is that my short stature got me roles. Pajamas were a fixture in my theatre-filled childhood.

I usually try to fit the experience or story to the question rather than focusing on a question and trying to find a story. As you explore ideas with students, it might be most useful to toggle between the two. Keep the questions in front of you while you listen for the story that might best fit one prompt.

With luck, the story may emerge early in the interview, but sometimes another meeting is necessary before the student feels ready to write. Students should feel ready to write when they know the story they want to tell and they have the prompt that goes with it.

When a student has difficulty finding a story, the mentor can go into the toolbox to find ways to generate material. I have some favorite "story starters" that I keep in my toolbox along with the information the student brings to our meeting, including:

- What is inside your desk?

- Tell me about what is hanging on the walls in your bedroom.

- What would I learn about you if you showed me the history of your Google searches?

- What is one thing in your closet you would never give away?

- What is on your playlist?

- Do you have a quote as a signature on your email? What is it and what does it mean to you?

- Describe a person who is the opposite of how you see yourself.

Here are two examples of responses to these questions:

WHAT IS INSIDE YOUR DESK?

What is on my desk at home? Issues of The Hockey News, *computer wires, and graph paper covered in derivatives can all be found strewn about my desk. There are also San Jose Sharks memorabilia, old theatre scripts and monologues leftover from classes and productions, and rulers and protractors. But my favorite items are all edible. I always keep a healthy supply of candy, to give me energy. I have strategically placed assorted candy in different hiding places inside my desk to make sure sweet-toothed thieves won't rob me of my entire stash. This security measure also serves as a system of both organization and self-control. I know I can find the Swedish Fish and the Gummi Worms in the back right corner of my desk; Smarties and lollipops are in the middle drawer; Hershey's Kisses, Mentos, and the Ghirardelli dark chocolates are in the drawer farthest to the left. Dark chocolate is my favorite, so I save it for the times when I have a workload emergency and I need to break out the chocolate reinforcements to keep me going. The big Ziploc bag of sunflower seeds can always be found on top of my desk. When I'm not feeling up to the caloric intake that comes with my candy, I turn to seeds. They're also my snack of choice when I have a free moment to watch my favorite TV shows on Netflix. I usually buy the biggest bag of regular, salted seeds and smaller bags of barbecue and ranch flavored seeds and put them all in a bag and shake it up. I get some joy from the surprise of which flavor might be coming next; the variety of flavors keeps things interesting. I love sunflower seeds because they give me something to do with my mouth but they don't actually fill me up, like junk food does. I am constantly filling my compost bin with shells of seeds, a sight that is either impressive or disgusting, depending on who you are. If someone were to find me sitting at my desk, being ultra-productive, they'd know that candy wrappers and a paper cup filled with shells weren't far away.*

This exercise gave me a lot of material to talk with the student about. I learned he loves hockey and enjoys both seeing plays and acting. I learned he's ultra-organized, but at the same time feels that he has to hide things from other people. He's worried about his health, but also about the environment, since I learned he composts at home.

WHAT WOULD WE FIND IF WE OPENED UP YOUR LAPTOP?

On my laptop you'd see a Google window open with many tabs. You would find Comedy Central open to the Daily Show's *latest episode. You would also find a few tabs open to Milton Friedman talks. I find his ideas fascinating; this man has certainly led me to develop an interest in economics. Pandora would certainly be playing. I love music-- any kind of music, from dub step to Mozart and almost everything in between, Justin Bieber aside. You would find Edmodo open, a website my school uses for teacher-student communication. I would be half-way through writing an email to my Key Club secretary organizing a fundraiser for Pediatric Trauma Prevention, while messaging my friend on Facebook about his thoughts on the latest Key and Peele video that I posted on his timeline. I truly think Key and Peele are comedic geniuses. You would find StumbleUpon open, a website that finds the best sites for you based on a survey taken when creating an account. I have read some of the most intriguing articles and I am always learning on this site. YouTube would be open to myriad Discovery Channel's "How It's Made" videos—like bubble gum or IMAX projectors. I would probably be partially done reading a witty article on the current election. I would have a Microsoft Word document open to an essay criticizing the Demographic Transition Model for IB Environmental Systems and Societies, and a tab open to Khan Academy reviewing related rates for a calculus test.*

Again, I learned a tremendous amount of information from asking this simple question. This student is clearly a multi-tasker who watches comedy while reading about economic theory! He has a deep sense of curiosity, enjoys satire, and always wanting to learn something new. He mentions an important club activity and his involvement in a fundraiser, as well as describing his tastes in music.

Aside from being fun questions to ask and easy for students to respond to, these questions actually reveal genuine information about each student's personality, what Dr. Gosling calls "décor-decoding: research." I use these questions to get students to talk about things they are comfortable with. Asking students to describe someone who they feel is the opposite of how they view themselves is much easier than talking about oneself. In Person Conceptualization research, students usually provide more elaborate descriptions of people they don't like—more so even than of people they do like or even a best friend. Apparently we think a lot more about why we don't like people than why we do, and those stories are easier to access.

These simple questions can get a shy student to start talking or help a reserved student to feel comfortable. Students often feel they have nothing "important" to say, so the mentor is needed to help the student weave these bits of information into something cohesive. The story starters are often a very successful technique to get a student talking, and then to get them writing.

Sometimes what you observe in the student can be reflected back to generate material. How do you feel interacting with the student? Is the student hilariously funny, dramatic, or entertaining? Does he dress distinctively or always carry a frightfully large backpack? Does he drink multiple cups of coffee in your office or raid your snack cabinet? Don't be afraid to reflect some of your own observations back to the student to see if a story might emerge.

I once worked with a student who attended an all-girls Catholic high school. She had a great sense of humor and was easy for me to interview. She did not have really distinctive extracurricular activities, and her paid job was as a recreation assistant. We struggled to find a unique storyline. Sometimes the storyline, however, is literally staring you in the face. On the day of our meeting, she came in late and wasn't in her school uniform. She explained she was late because she had wanted to stop at Starbucks after school, and that meant she had to change out of her school uniform. I asked her to repeat that statement, because it didn't make any sense. Why did she have to change her clothes to go to Starbucks? She proceeded to tell me this hysterical story about how her school would suspend students who went off campus wearing the uniform because they didn't trust the students to behave appropriately in public places and didn't want the public to be able to identify where the girls attended school. Her school was across the street from Starbucks, and every morning and every afternoon, dozens of girls could be seen in the parking lot, trunks opened, changing their clothes in public. This practice seemed to be sanctioned by the school, so long as the students didn't cross the street in their uniform.

I tossed the résumé aside and asked her several questions about the origin of the policy, how she felt about it, how it affected her daily life, and what she felt was hypocrisy by the administration. She wrote a funny and sentimental essay that started at the end: she was once suspended for wearing her school uniform at Starbucks. She then backtracked and wrote about being a campus ambassador who proudly wore her uniform at school as she escorted prospective students through the campus, but how she then wasn't trusted to drink her latté without damaging the reputation of the school. She ended the essay by stating how proud she would be to wear her college's logo all over her college town and to attend a school that trusted its students to represent the college well. She was able to write about her high school with humor and in a way that was critical but constructively so. The fact that she could tell this story comically made it work, and it was a perfect reflection of her personality.

One thing that is particularly challenging for the mentor is helping students re-frame their experiences or challenge what they tell you. I don't mean arguing with a student, but rather proposing an idea they have from a different point of view. This technique circles back to the earlier point of the mentorship: to help students reach beyond their current developmental level of social cognition.

For example, I worked with a student who was responding to a question about how she felt about diversity. In our interview, she discussed taking a class on world religion and how felt she knew a lot about different people from her teacher's lectures. I asked her if the teacher had brought in guest speakers from different cultural backgrounds to reflect on and share their experiences. He had not. The student's essay changed dramatically after we talked about what it meant to learn about diversity from one person's world view versus hearing and meeting with people who represented the cultures that were being discussed. The student realized, in fact, that she had learned much less about diversity than she had first thought. Her essay took the reader through her thought process of what it meant to actually know another person's life experience—one she now felt was limited by her teacher's decision to teach diversity through a single lens.

CHAPTER 6
ESSAYS FOR FITTING IN

Finding ways for students to explain their "fit" is often the most over-looked practice in essay writing and one which students might spend the least amount of time considering. But the fit is just as important to many schools as the student's ability to prove that he or she "stands out" amongst peers. It would seem reasonable that, at this point in a prospective student's college search, he or she would have thoroughly researched the colleges on his or her list and chosen them for reasons of "fit." I'm not merely referring to academic fit, of which students are probably quite aware—the average SAT scores of admitted students, the requisite high school course list, the median GPA, and maybe even whether the school has some majors the student may wish to study. But surprisingly few students know a lot about colleges beyond basic statistics such as the size of the campus and its reputation and location.

Not only does the college want to understand the personality of the student, but they also want the student to understand the personality of the campus. I often feel that students don't really take a look at the culture of a college until they are directly asked to in the college application. It's with good reason that some colleges require students to investigate their campuses more deeply before submitting an application—because they don't assume students will do that research on their own.

I worked with a student a few years ago who had spent much of her life in Africa. In her first essay, she wrote about her love for vast grasslands and open spaces and her need to be among wild animals. She wanted to use this essay to apply to the College of William and Mary, a school in a historically protected seventeenth-century corner of Colonial Williamsburg, Virginia. I suggested that her yearning for open space and views of free-roaming elephants weren't exactly a good fit for a college whose mission was to be a caretaker of the second oldest campus in America. With its distinctive history, William and Mary proudly states that they are the college of "American patriots, leaders, and public servants." The student wasn't necessarily a poor match for the academic rigor of the university, but had she submitted her original essay, the College may not have thought she'd be content spending four years on cobbled pathways amongst the tiny manicured gardens surrounding the campus. In the end, the student decided to attend the University of Vermont, where horses (though not elephants) roamed grass-covered hills. She had figured out her "fit."

All colleges may appear to offer the same majors, student living options, and social life, but through close examination of a school's website, along with discussions with current students and admission officers, prospective students will want to uncover the "values" of the college. A college's values are an important part of the student-to-college fit, and colleges often ask students directly in the application to describe how they fit the values of the campus community.

This process requires a lot of research into the college, its history, and how it views itself in its role to provide an undergraduate education. Students generally look first to choosing a college based on a variety of factors, including reputation or ranking, cost, location, academic offerings, and extracurricular activities. They may not care much about the hundred-plus years of traditions on which a college was founded, but the colleges care a lot. Each college thinks of itself as distinctive and wants to be sure a prospective student will appreciate that distinctiveness, or even seek it out. Students need to spend significant time researching colleges and discovering their unique qualities, in the same way the college will seek to discover the unique qualities of its applicants. In the application process, students may have no choice but to reflect on historic principles or contemporary values, and this is often where they gain confidence that they are choosing the right school for the right reasons.

Following are some examples of the descriptions of several schools' values as described in their mission statements, which can usually be found on their websites. These colleges all ask for supplement essays that ask applicants to reflect on the school's mission.

The differences in these three schools may seem subtle, but a student should carefully read through the mission statement and pull out phrases that carry special meaning or reflect his or her own beliefs. That statement or sentiment can then be reflected back to the college in the student's essay, clarifying to the college the strength of his or her fit.

The mentor can encourage the student to:

- Look for the Mission Statement on the website.

- Read about the history of the college.

- Read several issues of the school's student newspaper to find out what is currently happening on campus. (The student newspaper also provides the perspective of current students and may differ from material written on the admission website, which is usually written by their marketing department for the purposes of showing off the school's strengths.)

- Read the biographies of faculty in a department of interest. What research are they doing? What have they published?

Here is an example of a university's mission statement:

{ LOYOLA MARYMOUNT UNIVERSITY }

We benefit from our location in Los Angeles, a dynamic city that brings into sharp focus the issues of our time and provides an ideal context for study, research, creative work, and active engagement. By intention and philosophy, we invite men and women diverse in talents, interests, and cultural backgrounds to enrich our educational community and advance our mission:
- **The encouragement of learning**
- **The education of the whole person**
- **The service of faith and the promotion of justice**

The University is institutionally committed to Roman Catholicism and takes its fundamental inspiration from the combined heritage of the Jesuits, the Marymount Sisters, and the Sisters of St. Joseph of Orange. This Catholic identity and religious heritage distinguish LMU from other universities and provide touchstones for understanding our threefold mission.

A student doesn't have to tackle every piece of a school's mission statement in an essay, but the student should demonstrate why a mid-sized Catholic university in inner Los Angeles is the best fit for his or her personality and goals. Here is a student named Julia's essay, which does a fine job of reflecting on the school's mission:

I hope to attend LMU because LMU distinguishes itself as a school that not only offers rigorous academics, but also one that emphasizes the importance of social justice through its various programs organized by the campus ministry. I am seeking a college where I can also serve the society in which I will be living. The Service Retreat especially engages me. Social injustice is a global dilemma. However, I think that if we as a community want to address this problem, we need to begin with the problems close to home, which is why I am interested in the Service Retreat. I know that Los Angeles has one of the largest homeless populations within the United States, rather than protecting students from this sad reality, LMU actively encourages students to confront the issue by inviting them to learn about it and to stay over the weekend to provide meals for the homeless. I am currently involved in similar activities while in high school, and wish to continue that work in college. I want to be part of this Service Retreat and utilize this opportunity to be a contributor to society rather than to be just a consumer or just a student. I am also interested in your study abroad programs, especially those in Manila and El Salvador, as I have cultural roots in the Philippines and have studied Spanish for six years...

Julia clearly reflects specifically on LMU's mission and inserts some commentary on what she knows about the social issues in Los Angeles. She focuses on a specific program at LMU, which demonstrates that she has researched its many opportunities. Julia identified as Caucasian on the application, so she also used this opportunity to add that she is actually of mixed ethnic background and will contribute to the diversity of the student body.

{ DAVIDSON COLLEGE }

Davidson is an academically and socially engaged community bound by an Honor Code and committed to thoughtful discourse and an abiding sense of inclusiveness. Reflecting on your own background and educational experience, in what ways is Davidson a good match and how might you enrich this community?

In tackling this essay, the student should be clear about what the institution's honor code is and whether he or she would be able to adhere to it. The goal of this essay is to convince the admission committee that this student is a good fit for a liberal arts school in a small town in North Carolina that is committed to academic and social engagement. Here's is Rosie's essay, which does just that:

I love to learn. I want to be in an environment where I can talk about academics outside of the classroom—a place where everyone cares about what is going on in the world and has an opinion that they are eager to share. I am extremely interested in human nature and why people do what they do. This has sparked my interest in history and anthropology. In contrast, I am also fascinated with the scientific method and understanding how the world works in a physical sense. I am excited to get the chance to study all of these areas at Davidson. I know at Davidson I will also expand my academic interests.

I function well in a small classroom environment where I get the chance to voice my opinions and learn from all of my peers, along with the professor. I hold a tremendous amount of respect and admiration for enthusiastic teachers.

I have a liberal outlook and while I believe all humans have the capacity to be good, I also have a pessimistic view on the current direction society is headed. I believe that it is the responsibility of my generation to set society on the right course. I am excited to enter a community full of deep thinkers who will challenge and help me develop a point of view. My high school has a unique program called Small Learning Communities where students are divided up into houses for ninth and tenth grades. In their house, of approximately 100 students, they have the same history and English teachers both years. This program has deepened my interest in attending a small college because I can see that close relationships develop when students spend a lot of time together. As a member of the Davidson community I will bring my strong value for social justice and community service. This is why I want to get involved with the Chicken Soup Troup and eventually the Civic Engagement Council. I will also bring my creativity to both the classroom and to the Knitting Society. In addition, I hope to get the chance to continue developing my debating skills on the mock trial team and improving on my musical abilities with piano lessons. Lastly, I like to immerse myself in places full of history, to walk the same halls as people from over 170 years past who have upheld the Honor Code. I want to be in a school that is full of tradition, but is also constantly growing and changing as defined by its student body. I want to make an impact on what the future will see when they look back at my generation of Davidson students.

Rosie did a really nice job of responding to the college's historic traditions and its values of discourse and dialogue and providing examples of how she would engage at the university. I also like how she was able to explain the unique high school environment where she worked in small house communities. The college transcript is generally accompanied by a Secondary School Profile, a report the high school produces that describes their curriculum and student body. The college may have noted that she came from a non-traditional high school, but this essay gave Rosie the opportunity to reflect on her personal experience with the unique structure of the school.

.... * ....

{ THE UNIVERSITY OF CHICAGO }

Education is more than a set of skills, a rite of passage, or even the ability to think critically. It is an experience—part of a lifelong dialogue that encourages students to converse across cultures and disciplines—and is guided by 75 years of experience with a Core tradition . . . the goal is not just to transfer knowledge, but to raise fundamental questions and become familiar with the powerful ideas that shape our society.

The University of Chicago is known for its "core curriculum," which requires all students, regardless of major, to study physical sciences, social sciences, math, and humanities and to have competency in a foreign language. It is an academically rigorous school. A great response to this statement would illustrate an understanding of the school's attention to academic discipline, which Carmen achieved with her essay:

I've always had a specific idea of what "college" meant. The picture I have in my mind is one of a place where a person goes to learn something about everything, and more than something about one thing. It's a place where knowledge is acquired for its own sake, where you don't have to justify everything with an upcoming test or a grade. Most of all, it's a place where nobody knows anything for sure, and everyone is willing to learn from everyone else. The University of Chicago is the school that best exemplifies that idea of being unashamedly a student. The core curriculum seems designed to say, "You don't know this yet, but you should. Not because it looks good on a résumé, but because it's worth knowing." The more I learn, the more I realize how little I know, and UChicago understands that feeling, and seems to encourage it.

I also love the atmosphere of adventure, of trying new things. I already have an idea of what I want to do after college, but maybe I'll discover some area of study I never even dreamed of before, and follow that instead. And the adventure isn't just academic. I've spent the past eight years of my life on a synchronized swimming team. I loved it, because it taught me to appreciate the value of pushing yourself past your comfort zone. Since UChicago doesn't have a synchro team, but I still want to pursue athletics, I'm going to have to start a new sport, one I haven't played before. Since Chicago is a Division III school, there's less pressure to come into a sport you're already good at and stick to what you know. In other words, Chicago encourages its students to push past their boundaries, to try new things and explore. In sports, as well as in college in general, that's just what I'm looking for.

Carmen did her research on Chicago's core curriculum and let the school know that, while she had listed "pre-med" as her area of interest on her application, she wasn't going to complain about taking a philosophy course or a creative writing class. She appears confident and unconcerned about taking courses where she knows she will excel, and she even accepts the challenge of trying new things. She uses the values statement to elaborate on one of her extracurricular activities where she has the opportunity to acknowledge that she won't be able to continue in her sport, but she wants to remain an athlete and do so with the opportunities that The University of Chicago can provide. I like this essay because Carmen uses it as a jumping off point to provide a little more information about herself that wouldn't have had a place elsewhere in the application. She also referred to Chicago as "UChicago"—the shorthand that she would use once she was admitted.

Some colleges don't rely on the mission statement to look for "fit" but ask a general, "Why are you applying here?" I think these questions may appear easier to answer, but they don't push students to think as deeply or open the window for them to look in and see what the college wants them to see.

Here is an excerpt of a "Why___College?" essay response that was too general in its first draft and wouldn't easily convince a college that he or she had researched the school well and understood what made the college unique.

Draft 1: I have several interests that I'm thinking about studying in college; among them are psychology, health, and sociology. Given the many majors at your college, I would get a valuable education in any major I eventually will choose. Your college has the same gothic buildings of my high school and I know I will feel comfortable instantly on your campus. The college town surrounding the campus reminds me of my hometown. I love giving my opinion and learning from other students. Your small faculty and small class size will allow me to get to know my professors very well. I'd also like to study abroad and am happy to see all the programs you offer. I spent a semester in high school in England and enjoyed that experience.

This essay almost sounds like, "I'll like your college because it's feels comfortable." Most liberal arts colleges offer small classes and virtually every college has a study abroad program. This essay doesn't focus on any of the unique features of the college or reflect on its mission statement.

The student re-wrote the essay, including specific information on the study abroad program and adding information on the college's farm. She added information that gave more insight into her own values and how they matched the college's values of using the land and its geography as a place for learning. This student was awarded an $80,000 scholarship!

Draft 3: My favorite aspect about your college isn't just the gorgeous gothic campus, but the campus farm where students participate in growing the fruits and vegetables that are served in the dining hall. I like how students from all disciplines come together to work on the farm throughout the year and the value the college places on healthy lifestyles. The idea of eating fresh organic food everyday that is harvested by my classmates will inspire me to learn more about sustainable agriculture and its relationship to public health. I've never farmed before, but healthy living is important to me and I hope to use this experience outside of the classroom to learn more about improving health care in the United States. The study abroad opportunities offered at your college will also enhance my classroom studies. I'm extremely interested in having another opportunity to study in the United Kingdom with a homestay in Manchester, learning about the government system and the care of people with eating disorders. I would be very excited to have an internship experience with the National Health Service that is arranged through the college.

"Fit" and the Importance of College Visits

As students develop their college list, "fit" should be the guiding principle. Beyond the academic fit, students should be thinking about the cultural fit and the opportunities a college affords. While it's not always possible to visit every college on a student's list, students will find the "why?" question infinitely easier to write if they have engaged and connected with the campus through several points of contact prior to writing these essays.

For students who are unable to travel to campus, they can maintain communications with the admission officers, meet representatives and alumni at college fairs, and attend information sessions held in their hometowns. Reading the college newspaper regularly will inform them of issues and controversies that are happening on campus. These activities will help them learn more about what is distinctive about a college. Students can also e-mail professors to learn about the resources in an academic department, or read books professors have written.

A college visit is always helpful, but not if students race from campus to campus and miss out on spending quality time on campus to gain an in-depth look at the college. Concern may be unduly focused on the amenities of a college campus rather than the teaching and research opportunities. These aspects of the college will inform the student's experience more than the comfort of the extra-long mattress in the dorm or the convenience of the laundry room. A college visit that includes observing a class, meeting with faculty, attending a performance or symposium, and interviewing with admission officers, if possible, will give the student a treasure trove of material to write about.

CHAPTER 7

THE EDITING PROCESS: HOW TO EDIT WITHOUT A PEN

What does it mean for the writer to have the editor "edit without a pen"? Eventually a student's essay will be reviewed for proper grammar and spelling, but the role of the essay reader is to get the writer to the Better Essay by providing feedback that retains the essential structure, "voice," and style of the writer. Editing without a pen means to provide this feedback with a minimum of line editing by using techniques that allow the student the opportunity to self-edit.

In high school English classes, students are generally taught a very structured style of essay writing. Students writing the college essay may have just completed AP English Language and Composition in their junior year of high school, in which they are taught a prescribed style of writing with the goal of making rhetorical arguments, using text-based resources, and using quotes, summary, and paraphrase in developing their essays. Their final score on the AP exam reflects the effectiveness with which they use these devices. None of these devices help with the college essay, and editing for these devices isn't useful. In fact, students need to free themselves from this structure and draft an essay that greatly deviates from what they may have learned in school.

Voice

We use the term "voice" a lot when we talk about writing. Students hear this from their English teachers, and many students understand that their writing should reflect their voice. Sometimes they interpret voice as an opinion, but it's actually the voice that literally allows the reader to "hear" the student. Better Essays include word choices and cadence that help the reader feel like they are listening to the student. Important as it is for students to recognize their "voice," the mentor must also be equally respectful of it. When mentors edit with a pen or on a computer with Track Changes, the voice can easily turn into that of the mentor. An over-edited essay will not be reflective of the student's voice and may suspiciously not look like the student at all.

I received a phone call from one parent who was concerned that the short, choppy sentences of her student's essay would concern the admission office with its informality. Instead, I felt that the personality of the student really shined through. A city girl, Megan wrote like she talked. She is edgy, blunt, and terribly honest, with an underlying coat of humility and self-consciousness, all of which came through in her essay:

> *Lights shine into my face. Eyes heavy with fake lashes, skin caked with layers of foundation, mouth crusted with dark red lipstick. My body transforms into its paradoxical state: my naturally loose body seeks to maintain my character's stiffness. I am not Megan M. Murphy, a seventeen-year-old Irish-American high school student; I am Nikki Piganatelli, a weathered thirty-eight-year-old dance hall hostess and prostitute.*

> *Achieving this alternate persona was a journey of mental understanding and physical adaptation. I had to step out of my young, naive self and step into the skin of a woman with lost hope of love and happiness who sells her body to pay the rent.*

> *Flashback: Sweet Charity cast list: Megan Murphy . . . Nikki. I was ecstatic. Then the anxiety hit. How was I supposed to be Nikki? We are polar opposites—I am a teenager, a child—and Nikki is a woman. I find love and experience heartbreak; she hides from love and avoids men. I worry about getting grounded; she worries about returning to jail. How would I ever begin to understand and be this person?*

The Better Essay is free from a formal structure. The Better Essay can sound more like a very personal e-mail to a best friend than an essay written on *The Scarlet Letter*. It can feel chatty and informal. What's important is that the essay be free from prior writing constraints and written in a style that is easy to read and connects the reader to the writer in a distinctive manner—through interesting and varied vocabulary, details, and clarity. To keep the essay distinctive, it must retain the distinctiveness of the writer.

Word Currency

The words a student chooses can't be wasted on generic words that carry minimal meaning. They need to be seen as a currency that propels the essay forward and infuses more about the personality of the writer into the draft. A beloved second-grade teacher taught her students that words actually do have monetary value, and this concept has stuck with me in my own writing and has become a lesson I've passed on to others. She taught her young writers of penny words, dime words, and quarter words. When I'm reviewing a student's essay, I'll tell him or her the value I think a word has and I will mark the essay as such. The student's job is to replace the highlighted currency with a word or detail that increases its value. If there is space, the currency is increased with detail; if not, with a single word that packs more meaning.

Draft 1: And just like that, my diary became my safe haven. It was my place to share any and all ideas I had, even when I wasn't comfortable conveying them to the world. Most of the time, it was a way for me to keep a written record of my life. My theory was that I would always remember the big and meaningful events in my life, but I also wanted to remember the little things.

*Draft 2 (editor's comments): And just like that, my diary became my **dime**. It was my place to share any and **dime** I had, even when I wasn't comfortable conveying them to the world. Most of the time, it was a way for me to keep a written record of my life. My theory was that I would always remember the **penny** and **dime** events in my life, but I also wanted to remember **penny**.*

Draft 3: And just like that, my diary became my sanctuary. It was my place to share any and all emotions I had, even when I wasn't comfortable conveying them to the world. Most of the time, it was a way for me to keep a written record of my life. My theory was that I would always remember the formal rites of passage, receiving my Girl Scout Silver Award, and the day I passed my driver's test on the third try. But I also wanted to remember the ordinary times that brought me joy, such as getting a laugh out of my friends with my Seinfeld impersonations, or delivering my homemade jars of raspberry jam to my teachers at Christmastime.

Perhaps surprisingly, most students understand this simple concept and easily increase the value of their writing—usually without resorting to a thesaurus—just by thinking more broadly and deeply about what they're trying to convey. Once they understand the concept of word currency, they'll catch themselves and self-edit generic words: like, things, places, and feelings. They'll add details that are uniquely theirs and they'll become accustomed to considering the "value" of word choice.

Vocabulary Without a Thesaurus (Terms of Art)

An essay is interesting when it speaks to something very specific. It's not an opportunity to show off all the SAT words the student has memorized, but at the same time, the essay wants to convey some mastery of the English language. When students don't have a rich vocabulary, the tendency is to turn to a thesaurus. While it can be a useful tool, I encourage students to elevate the vocabulary quotient by inserting "terms of art" into the essay. That means a fisherman might know the complexities of fish, and a ballet dancer might have a rich dance vocabulary.

A granddaughter of a Holocaust survivor wrote the following essay using a few content-specific words: partisan, Resistance, Yom HaShoah. Her essay itself explains the words and their importance. The words then become integral to the essay and their meaning to the writer elevates the sense of authenticity.

What matters to you, and why?
_____

As a granddaughter of a Holocaust survivor, the remembrance of the Holocaust matters to me. I have always known that my grandmother lived through the Holocaust, and I grew up hearing stories about her life in Germany before she and her family were forced to escape in 1937. I understand how important it is to truly commit to the phrase "Never Again." Last year, as the President of the Jewish Club at Alameda Hills High School, I invited and arranged for a Holocaust survivor, a partisan, to speak to multiple classes at my high school. I chose to invite a partisan, a Jew who fought in the Resistance, because almost no one in the Jewish Club knew what a partisan was. My goal was to present a new perspective on the Holocaust that could not be fulfilled by studying famous Holocaust works such as Night *or* The Diary of Anne Frank. *For two years now, I have participated in the Bay Area Holocaust Memorial Service that takes place on Yom HaShoah, the day of destruction. I interview Holocaust survivors and read their stories to an audience of over a thousand people at this public memorial. Last year, I interviewed a ninety-eight-year-old man who escaped from Germany in 1936. I learned quickly that our meeting was really not an interview. He talked for a full hour without taking a break or giving me a chance to ask him questions. Afterwards, he invited my mother and me to have dinner with him. We agreed, and are still in contact with him, meeting him for dinner with his own family now and again. Perhaps this relationship came out of my willingness to just listen. I have noticed an eagerness from Holocaust survivors to tell their stories, as I've witnessed numerous testimonies at various memorial services. The more that we listen, the more it feels as if they become more at peace; that they are healing. By sharing their stories, by reminding us of the horrors they endured, we, the listeners, the next generation, can give the survivors peace of mind that their suffering will never be forgotten.*

Reading Out Loud

One very simple way to help students retain their voice (and I say "retain" because all students possess a voice) and not lose themselves in English-class rules is to have them read their essays aloud.

I use a dual-screen system with students. I have two monitors connected to a single computer. The student and I can sit across from each other and he or she can read me the essay while I follow along. When students "trip" on words, or stumble through sentences, it's a clear indication that they have lost their voice. Without even having to make a notation, the students will naturally change the sentence. When they hear the sentence aloud, it should flow from their mouth as if they were in conversation. They can usually instantly catch a sentence that took a wrong turn.

It might take a little prodding to get students to read their essays aloud. They might not be comfortable with the sound of their physical voice, or perhaps they have not been invited to read from their own work since early elementary school. They may feel somewhat embarrassed to present their work out loud. But eventually the students get used to this approach with the goal of self-correcting. Their editing, in this style, occurs naturally. Reading aloud also catches students who've looked up a few too many words in a thesaurus and can't pronounce the words on the page. Reading aloud requires them to focus on rhythm and pauses, prompting them to say, "I think that needs a comma," or, "My gosh, that's a long sentence." The written voice then easily edits itself when spoken.

DETAILS:

Draft 1: Whether playing drums or walking down the street I have music and am aware of my surroundings. I am in the moment. I am content. To me being content is when I am aware of myself and I exist where I am. I am not worried about what happened a second ago or what will happen in one second I am just there. This happens to me most often when I play the drums and relish in the music. It happens to me when I listen to music too, and even when all I have is the music in me. It is most prevalent however when I am playing music. When I play music I feel content and in the moment.

One of the things that students often lack is simply detail. In this essay, Albert talked about being aware of his surroundings. But what were his surroundings? I asked him to "take me there." I wanted to know what he was sensing, hearing, and feeling as he was walking down the street. Was he near the beach in Florida or in a busy metropolitan area? San Francisco or Providence? In order for Albert's essay to be distinctive, he needed to give the reader a sense of his place so that his voice grew from that environment. I'm not a musician, so I cannot surmise what it means to "have music in me." Albert's essay needed more explanation. I also asked Albert to add some music terms that might better convey the kind of music he loves. When students share the lexicon of their special interests, the sophistication grows without reliance on the thesaurus. It also infuses the essay with confidence and expertise.

QUESTIONS:
- What street?
- What were the surroundings?
- What else was happening at that moment?
- How do you make music without your instrument?

Draft 3: I groove, arms swinging, feet moving back and forth, as I walk home from school. The sidewalk is chipped and cracked. I walk through a residential neighborhood, then down a street with stores, and restaurants. Most days I would be listening to my iPod through headphones. Today however, I forgot them at my house. It's okay though because I still have music with me—music is always with me. I constantly compose and play in my head. I am a jazz musician and I am most content composing and playing music. As I keep walking, the yell of a delivery man at the Chinese supermarket overlays with the sensation of my shoes on the pavement. I respond, pulling my hand out of my pocket and cracking my knuckles. This dialogue is typical in jazz—a call and response, back and forth. The sounds surrounding me combine and fall away making room for the next musical sequence. I find music everywhere in my life.

There is the "personal voice" in writing—the writing that sounds like it comes from the mouth of the student in his or her "accent," so to speak, which is as unique as the student. But there is another voice to bear in mind as well, the "literary voice," which shows whether the subject of a sentence acts (active voice) or is acted upon (passive voice).

ACTIVE VOICE: the subject **PERFORMS** the action of the verb.

PASSIVE VOICE: the subject **RECEIVES** the action of the verb.

Active voice is almost always superior to passive voice because it makes for stronger, clearer sentences.

EXAMPLES:

1. The pizza was eaten by the students. (passive)

   should read . . .

   The students ate the pizza. (active)

2. The movie was watched by a large crowd. (passive)

   should read . . .

   A large crowd watched the movie. (active)

3. A glowing review was written by the critic. (passive)

   should read . . .

   The critic wrote a glowing review. (active)

A few sentences of passive voice may be acceptable, particularly when it is necessary to convey a specific point of view. For example, *the cat was chased by the dog* describes the cat's experience, whereas *the dog chased the cat* describes the dog's experience. But for the most part, active voice should be favored.

Students should be able to identify when they are using active and passive voice. As the reader, be sure to highlight any sentences written in passive voice and see if an active voice that puts the subject in control will improve the essay.

Word Count

In the movie *Amadeus*, this famous exchange occurs between the brilliant Mozart and the Austrian Emperor:

EMPEROR: My dear, young man, don't take it too hard. Your work is ingenious. It's quality work. And there are simply too many notes, that's all. Cut a few and it will be perfect.

MOZART: Which few did you have in mind, Majesty?

EMPEROR: Well. There it is.

In this humorous exchange, the Emperor found Mozart's work too rich, but he couldn't be specific as to what could be cut and still retain the beauty of the music. Despite the Emperor's opinion, Mozart was free to include as many notes as he wanted. One of the greatest challenges for college essay writers is that there is almost always a word limit. While writing the Common Application essay at 650 words or less, or supplemental or college-specific essays, which tend to be around 300 to 350 words, it's often difficult for students to stay under the word count in a first draft. It takes a lot of experience as a writer to have a natural sense of word count. As ideas flow, so do words. In my work with students, I provide them with these three rules:

1. The goal is to come as close to the maximum as possible. Colleges choose a word count because they expect an essay of a particular length—not too little and not too much. Writing too briefly could indicate lack of effort. Too long an essay may be literally "cut out" of the computer once the student hits the maximum, or demonstrate a lack of focus and a lot of rambling.

2. The initial draft should be no longer than 100 words over the count for a long essay of 500 to 650 words and no more than fifty words longer than a short essay of 300 to 350 words. The essay reader shouldn't have to wade through a draft that is so far off the mark in length that large chunks would have to be cut, and the writer needs to maintain awareness of the word count during drafting.

3. When the essay is submitted to the reader, it should state the word count at the top of the page so the reader starts off with the knowledge of whether the essay is a bit too long or a bit too short.

Editing for Length: Word Compacting

Helping the student achieve the word limit or turn a long essay into a shorter essay for a different prompt requires the essay to stay true to its theme and structure. This shortening can often be accomplished by "word compacting." Word compacting means shortening a sentence without distorting its meaning by finding a single word that means the same as several words, or altering the sentence structure. For example, this essay had a 350-word requirement. Dustin's first draft came in too long. To help students learn to compact their own essays, the mentor can give students sample essays that are fifty to 100 words too long and ask them to re-write the essay within the word limit. Students can compare the new versions of the essay, analyzing which samples are closest to the original structure and retain as much of the same information as possible.

{ DRAFT 1 }

396 words (350-word limit)

Describe your intellectual interests, their evolution, and what makes them exciting to you. Tell us how you will utilize the academic programs in the College of Arts and Sciences to further explore your interests, intended major, or field of study.

I am currently undecided about what I want to study, but I am especially interested in sociology, government and psychology.

Cornell's offerings in the Sociology Department would allow me to investigate questions I have and areas that I'm interested in, particularly popular culture and societal trends. I'm somewhat of a pop-culture junkie, so I'd love to learn more about the science behind popular culture and the evolution of people and the way they interact. In addition to general sociology, Assistant Professor Matthew Brashears' interests in both social psychology and political sociology also intrigue me. I would love to learn more about his experience uncovering "covert social networks" in the Covert Social Network Project and how that is relevant to my interests in societal trends and popular culture. This project is unique to Cornell, and I think it would provide invaluable experience working with sociological ideas.

My interest in government and politics, too, has really grown this past semester in the heat of the presidential election. Assistant Professor Adam Levine, in the Government Department, specializes in "political context" and political behavior. This interdisciplinary interest is perfect for me and is just another great feature of Cornell, as I could study both constitutional politics and the sociological side of politics. To further fulfill my interest in government, Cornell in Washington really caught my eye because I would be able to get the full experience of Cornell on campus and also have the opportunity to spend a semester in the thick of the political scene in Washington, DC. I would love to take advantage of this unique opportunity and many more at Cornell.

Finally, Cornell's Psychology Department is incredibly attractive to me because of its interdisciplinary concentrations. The Social and Personality Psychology concentration provides perfect overlap between sociology and psychology, which I would love to take advantage of. I am also very interested in neuroscience because of an Advanced Topics in Biology class, which is a modified version of AP Biology, which I took during my junior year. Another concentration of Cornell's Psychology Department, the Behavioral and Evolutionary Neuroscience concentration, would allow me to further explore both psychology and neuroscience (and its relation to psychology).

Cornell's opportunities for interdisciplinary studies and unique Cornell in Washington program would be perfect for me, as I would be able to explore many different subjects and ultimately find one that I will pursue.

{ FINAL DRAFT }
346 words (350-word limit)

I am undecided about what I want to study, but I am especially interested in sociology, government and psychology.

Cornell's offerings in the Sociology Department would allow me to investigate questions particularly in the area of popular culture and societal trends. I'm somewhat of a pop-culture junkie, so I'd love to learn more about the science behind popular culture, the evolution of people, and their interactions. In addition to general sociology, Assistant Professor Matthew Brashears' interests in both social psychology and political sociology intrigue me. I'd love to learn more about his experience in the Covert Social Network Project and how that relates to my interests in societal trends *and popular culture. This project is unique to Cornell, and will provide me invaluable experience working with sociological ideas.*

My interest in government and politics has really grown this past semester in the heat of the presidential election. Assistant Professor Adam Levine (Government Department) specializes in "political context" and political behavior. This interdisciplinary interest is perfect for me and is just another great feature of Cornell, as I could study both constitutional politics and the sociological side of politics. Cornell in Washington really caught my eye because I would be able to get the full experience of Cornell on campus and also have the opportunity to spend a semester in the thick of the political scene in DC. I would love to take advantage of this unique opportunity and many more at Cornell.

Finally, Cornell's Psychology Department is incredibly attractive to me because of its interdisciplinary concentrations. I could take advantage of the Social and Personality Psychology concentration—the perfect overlap between sociology and psychology. I am also very interested in neuroscience, developed in my junior year in Advanced Topics in Biology class. Another concentration of Cornell's Psychology Department, Behavioral and Evolutionary Neuroscience, would allow me to further explore both psychology and neuroscience.

Cornell's opportunities for interdisciplinary studies and unique Cornell in Washington program would be perfect for me, as I would be able to explore many different subjects and ultimately find one that I will pursue.

Content and the Hook

The hook, another term familiar to students, means engaging the reader in the first few opening sentences. Engaging a reader is an essential element of the college essay, but it's a focus of the entire essay, not a few sentences. If the voice is present, that alone can engage the reader, and as the story unfolds, the reader is compelled to continue reading. So a hook can capture interest in the first few sentences, but it's not the most important element of that essay. The hook doesn't imply supreme importance—you've caught the reader's attention, so now you've engaged him or her and what follows doesn't have to be as interesting. Instead, the Better Essay engages the reader from the start and continues to engage throughout. Clarity is also essential at the beginning of the essay. If I don't understand where the essay is going in the first several sentences and I'm tired or distracted or overwhelmed with a pile of essays to read, I may just stop reading.

{ Draft 1 }

Students should describe the world they come from—for example, their family, community, or school—and tell the reader how their world has shaped their dreams and aspirations.

In this essay, the student, named Navashen, begins with a "hook" describing the colors of chalk at a festival.

The grass stained purple, orange, with a splash of yellow, and finally a blotch of red. Holi, the Indian festival of colors, was now over. I admitted to my parents that it was a unique experience, although I didn't exactly know why we had to throw colored powder around. Laughing, my mom depicted how the festival would be larger and more exciting with all my relatives back in India. This topic had come up before. Not just for Holi but for other aspects of my life as well. I was celebrating a festival whose origins I did not know, and celebrating without the people I was supposed to be with.

My lack of knowledge of my own heritage produced a strange disconnection. The fact that I have been going to different Indian festivals and events and not knowing its history seemed wrong as I had been to these events as long I could remember. It was like going to someone's birthday party and not knowing what it was for. Even with this lack of insight, I still won't be able to enjoy these eventful days with kin, most of whom I've never met or got to bond with.

Even though most of us don't have many relatives in the community to celebrate with, people still have the will to set up festivals for the community. Maybe they want their children to experience and appreciate their previous heritage and hope that they will keep the traditions in future generations. I hope these efforts made an impact, so others can stray away from my predicament of ignorance and isolation. Hopefully others in this generation will strive to not only enjoy, but also understand the significance of these festivals and will try to celebrate them with extended family.

While Holi celebrations reflected cultural tradition, these attempts were artificial replications of the true experiences that one would witness in India. Yes, the ideologies and intent are the same, but the celebrations that are created here lack the distinct familial environment while living in India. For one I would like to go to India for Holi, Diwali, or any other holiday to enjoy the real experience. It is the fusion of the cultural holiday with the moments celebrated with brothers, sisters, cousins, and friends alike that make the Indian holidays what they are.

Navashen started with a good hook, but the content strayed away from his personal experiences quite quickly. He wrote this essay with an emphasis on what "other" people gain from these holiday celebrations. He was almost absent entirely in the third paragraph, and his conclusion was written in the third person. I wanted to know more about his background and the context of these celebrations. I wanted him to answer the question clearly: what are *your* dreams and aspirations?

QUESTIONS:

- Where was this event held?

- How often have you celebrated Holi?

- How many people were there? Just family, or others? Did you know them?

- Why had no one told you what the festival meant? What was the purpose of your attending?

- How did this holiday compare with celebrating American holidays?

- Have you been to India before?

- What are your "dreams and aspirations" about understanding your identity?

{ Draft 3 }

The grass stained purple, orange, with a splash of yellow, and finally a blotch of red at Hamilton Square Park in Jersey City. Holi, the Hindu festival of colors, was now over and all 150 attendees started to clean, pack up, and head home. My family was completely covered in colored powder and we laughed together. But later, I admitted to my parents that I didn't exactly know why we had to throw colored powder around, even though this was the third Holi festival I had attended. It felt strange that I had no idea what significance the festival carried.

My parents said that they wanted me to experience what Hindu culture was about, but for me, there was no emotional connection. There is nothing to long for. During my childhood, the values behind these festivals were barely discussed; when I was younger my parents shared some children's books about Hindi culture, but I hardly remember these stories. The same went for American holidays such as Christmas and Thanksgiving. We gave each other presents, bought turkeys, but never attained the holiday spirit itself. I essentially celebrate two cultures indifferently.

I am not exactly sure why my parents never celebrated either American or Indian traditions fully. Maybe they know that I am Americanized and would celebrate American holidays anyway, as we do occasionally with family friends. However I feel that these celebrations are just parties rather than actual holiday celebrations. I believe they wanted to keep my Hindu culture alive, as we always buy traditional clothes and food when we go to visit India. Unfortunately the timing of these trips never coincided with major festivals that occur much earlier and later in the year. In any case, these visits didn't teach me about Hindi culture; they were about visiting relatives. Therefore, I haven't yet truly developed a devoted cultural identity or experienced the anticipation and excitement of an approaching holiday.

My life is currently empty of cultural significance, experiences that most people have and take for granted. Now that I understand what I have missed, I want to actively fill this emptiness. I can experience these Hindu festivals personally in India, in order to appreciate the scale and significance of my Hindu legacy. If I am truly Americanized, I can fully embrace the meaning behind American holidays with set customary traditions and make them something that I can relate to and look forward to. Maybe since I'm not biased towards one culture, I will be able to develop both American and Hindu traditions equally. I may not develop both cultures fully, but developing cultural values will be a lifelong endeavor.

Tips for Sharing Drafts

As the college essay mentor, you're going to be reading a lot of material. Establishing a system for receiving and replying to drafts is essential for both the individual student you are helping and for keeping track of multiple students' work. Using a simple system that allows each draft of an essay to be retained for future reference makes it possible to go back to themes or ideas that might have been taken out of earlier drafts. As different essay themes may be re-used for different prompts, there is a constant process of customizing material. Losing earlier drafts in original formats makes the task much more difficult. While one college may ask for a 500-word essay on a theme, another may ask for the same response with a 300-word limit. If, in the editing process, the student makes changes but doesn't retain all versions, he or she might have to do additional work when new prompts appear. Relying on Google Docs or other file-sharing systems such as Dropbox may help.

Using a simple number system is another way to be efficient, keep track of all drafts, and retain the flexibility to move between essays.

1. Students should number all drafts with ODD NUMBERS.

2. Each draft should include:

    a. Student's name.

    b. Where the application is going:

        i. Application form (Common App, Universal, school-specific)

        ii. Name of college

        iii. Essay question completely written out

        iv. Draft #

        v. Word count of document/word limit of essay

3. Mentors should mark all replies, suggestions, and comments, which will appear on a new draft renumbered with EVEN NUMBERS.

4. Whether the drafts are sent by e-mail or some other electronic method or prepared in printed form for review, a numbering system or similar code prevents loss of work and easy reference.

5. Supplement essays should be included in a single document. Some schools have two or more supplemental questions. Reviewing them all in a single document allows the reader to make sure there are no inconsistencies or redundancies in responses. Even if a student has not yet completed all the questions and wants the reader to respond to a partially written supplement section, all the questions should appear in one document. The single document also makes revising, reviewing, and keeping track of drafts much simpler. This document should include:

   a. Name of student

   b. Name of school

   c. Draft # (odd)

   d. Fully written supplemental questions

   e. Word count of essay/word limit of essay

The Importance of the Mentor in the Editing Process

Editing without a pen means engaging the student in the editing process by asking meaningful questions to help him or her expand on or reshape an idea and providing feedback on what is clear and what is vague. It also means providing students with tools so that they become better editors of their own work. I feel very strongly that the feedback should be from the mentor to the student, and peer to peer editing should always be avoided. While it is tempting to ask students in a classroom or small group to provide feedback to their peers, it will undoubtedly cause students to be less open in their writing. If students know that other students will read their work, they may not feel open to express these very personal thoughts and experiences. Additionally, high school students typically are not experts at either line-editing or on the expectations of the college essay. For the essays to truly become Better Essays, the mentors need to stick with the student from brainstorming to the final draft.

CHAPTER 8

FACING CHALLENGES: WHEN YOU CAN'T GET GOING ON A THEME

A student living in New Zealand submitted a series of essay drafts to me over the course of one summer. Each draft had bits and pieces of her fascinating internship working alongside a veterinarian who cared for large mammals. I returned each draft to her with my list of questions and suggestions of what to take out and what to leave in. Finally, instead of submitting a formal draft, Harper wrote me a very long e-mail. It started with, "What I'm trying to say is . . . "

"Harper," I replied after reading her message, "you just did."

When Harper stopped staring at a blank computer screen and felt she was telling me a story through letter writing, her essay evolved naturally. Simply by putting on a different writer's hat, so to speak, she communicated exactly what she couldn't in an "essay." With students who are meeting with me in person, they may talk while I record their words and phrases on paper. I often record the story and give the student the recording to transcribe.

Students can get tangled up in the structure of a formal piece of writing. Formality will interfere with the narrative and trap them in unexpected ways. Sticking to an outline might work well for an essay on the debate of the WikiLeaks controversy, but the dynamic college essay requires free-flowing thoughts. Storytelling calls for a schematic approach. While an outline is a linear process that begins with large topics broken down into smaller components, storytelling often begins midway, backtracks to a plot, and sets up the temporal relationships between character and events.

We have all had the experience of listening to someone tell a dull story, where the plot is slow to unfold and we have no idea where the story is going or how the characters are related to each other. We may be unable to conjure up the backdrop of the story. We may simply be told a recanting of a chronology of events. The teller may feel the punch line at the end will tie the story together, but the listener may have already drifted away. A story that starts towards the middle, works back to the beginning, and completes the circle with an event that draws meaning can be much more captivating.

In one adaptation of *Cinderella*, we meet the title character sitting amongst the ashes in her cottage. Her stepsisters and stepmother enter. We later learn that Cinderella's father had died and she was left to labor for this wicked family he had married into after the early death of Cinderella's mother. Cinderella then heads off to the ball at the palace with the help of her fairy godmother. In the end, the prince arrives at Cinderella's modest home, searching for the maiden who lost a glass slipper at the ball. Back in Cinderella's chair beside the fireplace, the prince discovers that Cinderella is the woman he loves.

This version of *Cinderella* doesn't begin when she was born, or when her mother died and her father remarried. It begins in the middle of Cinderella's current plight—with what is on her mind at that very moment we meet her. We learn later of her history and the relationships between the characters, and we then embark with Cinderella on her adventure. The story closes with the return to the literal place where the story began, in Cinderella's home. This simple fairy tale provides a good example of the structure of a narrative.

Sometimes simply inviting the student to tell the essay rather than write the essay will cause it to miraculously appear.

Here is an initial draft, by a student named Jordan, that had that "in the beginning" feel:

Draft 1: After I was accepted to the Majesty School (an institution that blends traditional academics with musical education) in fourth grade, I needed to choose a string instrument to learn. The Director of Admissions looked at me and immediately said I was a bass player. After one lesson I was hooked. As a double bassist, I rarely get to be the star of any group. However, as a young middle school bassist I thought that I ought to be heard. My private bass instructor used to tell me that I needed to stop being the "bull in the china shop." Being a young music student, I reluctantly took this advice. As I entered high school, I thought jazz would be an opportunity for me to be the star.

I asked Jordan just two questions.

1. How do you get that bass into your car for lessons?

2. Why did Majesty School think you should be a bass player?

When this student answered my questions, his story emerged. He started with the here and now, and then backtracked to the beginning.

Draft 3: I don't know how I manage to fit a bass, two amps, several music stands, and piles of sheet music into my Prius. I don't know how I even fit all six-foot-three, 230 pounds of me into a Prius every week when I'm off to rehearsals. I've been lugging this bass around since third grade when I entered the Majesty School, a selective music and academic school. I auditioned on piano but I was asked to switch to bass as soon as the Admissions Director looked at me and took note of my height. At Majesty, I did learn how to play the bass, but I did not truly learn what it meant to be a bassist until much later.

Challenges in writing the essay come about in other forms. They can come from a student who is intent on being dramatic, or one who feels a need to itemize the chronology of an experience that seems too familiar to the reader. The essay can seem a challenge to write when a student feels her life was uneventful, or if she has identified learning challenges that are deemed the core of her identity. I've also found that students need direction in researching ideas for some categorical essays.

Writing With Rapunzel

There are many students who have had lives of adventure and travel or who have an intense passion for sports or the arts, interesting families and jobs, or other amazing insights. Eagle Scouts seem always to have stories at hand of winter storms on mountain tops and pitching tents in the dark without tools. Then there are students who have had little experience with life outside of school—and even within their everyday life, there may be little, it seems, to draw upon. These students might face the dynamic essay with particular dread, sensing they aren't up to the task of developing an interesting narrative. But I believe that everyone has a story to tell. Affluence, whether cultural or economic, does not have the corner on great storytelling.

I once worked with a student I'll refer to as Rapunzel. She lived in a glorious home surrounded by vineyards, but her life was pretty lonely. She had no hobbies, no friends, and a family that left her mostly alone with her computer, where she entered chat rooms for company. At nineteen, she had never passed her driver's test and she lived in such a remote area that she couldn't get to town on her own, even on a bike or by foot. But her kitchen window provided the literal view for an interesting essay—and so it was that it became the topic. She wrote about the landscape beyond that window and her time spent sketching it. In her isolation, she paid particular attention to the plants and trees in her yard, how they changed color with the seasons, how they climbed along the stone walls that surrounded her home. Without knowing her background, it was easy to infer that she had an eye for nature and beauty, and her expressed interest in botany felt authentic.

Another student who lived on the water and had an interest in marine biology similarly wrote a compelling essay about the rowboat at his back door and his sunrise rides through the wide canals around his home. He had yet to dive into the ocean, but his essay was a convincing testimony to his desire to venture to places yet to be discovered.

Word Poverty

The term "word poverty" has been used to describe students from linguistically poor backgrounds whose vocabulary, compared to more affluent peers with college-educated parents, is already three million words fewer than their peers by the time they are four years old. In Chapter 7, we discussed Terms of Art. I believe that students can unleash a rich vocabulary by focusing on what they know well. Whether it's church rituals or street games, a smattering of foreign expressions and their meanings, or the language of food, bus routes, bicycles, or their city streets, no college essay need be impoverished by a lack of interesting words. The task for the mentor is to help students reveal that vocabulary in their writing.

In group settings, teachers and mentors can make a game of asking students to write down on index cards the words they think are their own secret vocabulary, or words shared only within their home, on their street, in their sports club, or in their religious community. Swapping index cards of words and awarding points for the words no one can guess can help students feel enriched rather than impoverished by a lack of formal "school" words.

A student named Michael had dyslexia and a limited written vocabulary but was an expert fisherman. Using his knowledge of procuring salmon, he wrote this essay on his third draft. It was full of the spelling errors emblematic of some students with dyslexia, but those were easy to correct.

We can't fit one hundred pounts of fish in our freezer. We had to religh on my grand-pa's freezer, the kind you would grab an ice cream from at the local delle.

Armed with two, Two feet by two feet, by three feet boxes filled with salmon and halibut packed with dryed ice, we were on our last day of our Alaskan fishing trips ready to check our luggage and fish on to the plain. Ever since I was nine I have been going fly fishing with my dad, and out of the many adventurs we have gone on our trip to Alaska was my most memorable.

Our goal when we left home was to bring as much Silver salmon home as posable. Although you could buy silver salmon at the grosry store, there is always a more sat-isfying feeling when you know you caught the fish you are eating. When we were on the river, there were two kinds of salmon, silver salmon and pink salmon. Catching a silver in the vast pods of pinks is like trying to see an eagle is a flock of crows. My father and I sat in a boat in temperatures that felt like winter to try and catch fresh fish not only for the delitious meal that would fallow but also for the excitement and rush we get when a fish is at the end of our line.

Michael's first draft referenced a freezer where the fish were stored. Realizing that the amount of fish Michael caught couldn't fit within a standard kitchen freezer, I asked Michael to describe it. When he said, "Like the kind you get your ice cream bar from at the delicatessen," I told him to include that expansion into his essay. It provided an important visual and gave the reader a sense of the size of his catch. He didn't know the word "commercial," but he could describe it. I loved his phrase, *"Catching a silver in the vast pods of pinks is like trying to see an eagle in a flock of crows."* He may have heard that phrase many times from his father, or he may have invented it for this story, but regard-less, it was eloquent and demonstrated his knowledge of the sport of fishing.

Backseat to a Learning Difference

Almost every student I have worked with who has had a diagnosis of dyslexia, ADHD, or some other learning difference has had the experience of struggling in school, rounds of testing and re-testing, and ultimately a label that relieved the students of some personal guilt for the immense effort it took them to succeed in school. The essays in which these students write about their learning differences are honest, but they tend not to differentiate themselves from students who have had similar struggles. In addition, there is space on college applications to explain special circumstances or academic challenges, so the dynamic essay does not need to be used for the purpose of explaining educational history, although it can be embedded into a story focusing on other aspects of the students' lives. It is my hope for these students, as well, that they don't define themselves solely by a diagnosis. I hope that as they leave high school they will see the learning difference as one aspect of themselves and can use the college essay to reflect upon the learning difference as a matter of fact—something that has been part of their life but not consumed by it.

A typical draft might look like this:

Every year in school seemed to get harder and harder. I had no idea why. Was it the homework load? Was I just getting dumber by the day? Ever since kindergarten I was always in trouble for not paying attention—remarks of the like seemed always to appear on my report card. By the time tenth grade came around, the schoolwork was crushing me and I asked my parents for an evaluation. It was odd that they hadn't thought of that before. When I got the diagnosis of ADHD I was devastated. I thought that meant I was stupid. It took a lot of education to realize that my intelligence wasn't related to the ADHD. It just meant I had to work differently in school and learn to let the support team at school help me organize my work more efficiently.

A Better Essay might integrate a diagnosis into the whole person so that the reader has the opportunity to learn about the student who lives with a diagnosis, not in spite of one. The following essay demonstrates how seamlessly this art student briefly mentions ADHD in her response to a Topic of Choice prompt. Her ADHD even helps us understand her artistic drive more fully:

Now, as a senior in high school, I am very interested in possibly pursuing a career in art. My work consists of mostly paintings, each composed of different mediums, such as watercolor, acrylic, and oil. A lot of my paintings currently involve figures or people because I am practicing my anatomy drawing. For example, I created a portrait of a woman in the style of artist Egon Schiele and this is one of my favorite paintings to date. I also do a lot of sketching that consists mostly of still life objects, but also imaginative drawings. What drives me to make art is being in control of something totally original and unique in my own personal way. As a kid with an ADHD diagnosis there were times of struggle, and art was an outlet for me. In a way, creating art was my savior, passion, and therapeutic way of dealing with any situation that was thrown at me, and made me a stronger, more expressive person. Even when I was young, I would imagine a concept and that dart in my mind pinpointed an idea. I'd get a rush of adrenaline and immediately start working and completely immerse myself into the project. The feeling is indescribable, but it's almost supernatural and it feels like I've entered my own space where anything is possible.

Focus on the Here and Now

Helping students with weaknesses in language is possible with techniques used by speech and language therapists, such as therapeutic storytelling techniques, which can improve literacy and pragmatic language. As speech therapist Teresa Cherry-Cruz wrote, "Storytelling opens the door for an introduction to story grammar, where students can walk through stories and learn about settings, characters, problems, plans, consequence, and reaction. These types of story walks can easily be converted to activities of reading and writing."

Having students practice storytelling as a routine classroom activity using their own or published material will prepare students for the narrative task of writing the college essay. Improvisational storytelling, for example—such as having students create stories for each other using four prompts: a person, place, time, and a "wild card" word—can get students into the spirit of storytelling. This activity can help a group of students develop the structure of imaginary stories that can be helpful in developing their own narratives.

A student with significant learning and processing challenges may be given the assignment for the college essay of engaging in an activity and then immediately telling the story into a tape recorder, for later transcription.

For one such student with significant learning and processing challenges, it was hard for her to recall the details of past experiences that would have created a deeply introspective essay.

She had been studying American Sign Language at school, an option given to students with learning differences. I asked Zabie if she had ever met a Deaf person. She hadn't, but she told me she heard there was a restaurant in a nearby city that was owned by a Deaf family where all the wait staff used sign language.

I asked the student to go to the restaurant along with a classmate, and when she returned, to immediately dictate her story into a tape recorder so she could transcribe it later. Again, this student was able to mention the learning difference as a part her life, but not the focus of her being. Her task was not to try to be introspective, to relate disparate experiences, or to recall and integrate past experiences. By focusing on the here and now, the student was able to craft a sweet and funny story:

I rarely drive to San Francisco even though it is only thirty minutes from my home. However, I had a goal to go and practice my signing skills at a restaurant in San Francisco. I have dyslexia and learning has always been a challenge for me. I thought American Sign Language (ASL) would be the best choice for my language requirement. I am a visual and kinesthetic learner and have been taking ASL classes at my high school for three years.

Walking several blocks through the City to the Mission District after having searched for parking, my friend Sara and I arrived at our destination, Restaurant Mozzeria. I was excited and nervous about utilizing my ASL skills. I had never communicated with a Deaf person and was excited to see how my classroom experience would translate to the real world. My ASL teacher at school is partially deaf and forms words from her mouth, making it fairly easy to understand her.

The Italian restaurant was a modern-styled intimate setting and the city's first Deaf-owned restaurant. Upon arrival, we were greeted by a Deaf hostess. The owners and all of the employees are also Deaf. Our waiter, Aiden, whose name was embroidered onto his shirt, presented us with a smile and a note that said he was Deaf and happy we were here and happy to serve us. Prior to ordering, Sara and I began signing to each other in preparation of conversing with Aiden. We laughed when we forgot some basic signs.

Fortunately, when Aiden asked for our order I was able to sign that I "need more time." Upon ordering I was pleasantly surprised with my ability to ask a question. I had asked Aiden the sign for "duck" by finger spelling "D-U-C-K." Then I was able to ask if it was spicy. I decided on the potato gnocchi and it was delicious. During the meal I asked Aiden for more water and later for the check.

Most of the other customers were also signing and it felt good to include myself in what had now become the norm. We noticed that some of the customers were Deaf. Aiden presented us with the check and wrote a note that read, "Keep studying ASL."

Intent to Be Dramatic

In their effort to stand out, students may confuse the essay with a "tell-all" of every crisis in their life, or with the intent to create a dramatic version of a normal teenage life. Working with one particular student who felt the need for drama, I received essay after essay of escalating crises. With each draft I tried to figure out what she wanted to say to the admission office. "What do you want them to infer?" I asked Trinity. "I want to stand out," she insisted.

Everyone in my 92nd Street Y Musical Theater Camp was waiting patiently for the casting results. Our teachers had been outside debating who would play whom in our fourth grade production of A Little Shop of Horrors *for what seemed like forever. I was dead-set on playing Audrey, the beautiful female lead who gets to both fall in love and die over the course of the show. No one else deserved the part more than me. I had practiced her songs over and over again for our audition. I even started memorizing some of her lines in the script.*

Finally, our teachers came out and began announcing the parts one by one. "Audrey," they said, and I held my breath, "will be played by . . . Natalie." I felt my stomach plummet. I heard my teacher continue, "Mr. Mushnik will be played by . . . Trinity." In that moment, I could have died. Not only did I not get to play the role that I was born to play, but I had to play Mr. Mushnik, a fifty-year-old fat man. It didn't matter that it was a large role. It was the wrong role, and I knew why I was stuck with it too.

There aren't very many boys in musical theater, so ever since I decided to cut my long hair when I was seven, I had to play all of the boys' parts. Girls like Natalie who were skinny with long, blonde hair would beat me for the good parts every time. I was sick of being labeled as masculine just because of my hair-cut, glasses, and strong build. I decided that I would have to grow out my hair in order to compete with the other girls.

My suggestions and efforts to lead her to a less dramatic and angry version of herself were futile, until I tried something I had never tried before. I called her, feeling quite desperate to get a Better Essay before she impulsively sent off something I felt would make her seem, at best, egocentric. With this student, I actually encouraged her to write something boring, in an attempt to counterbalance her overly exaggerated narrative.

"Trinity," I said, "write me the most boring essay you can. Make me fall asleep with details of your daily life. No drama, no angst, no urgency. Take me from your home to your acting class in the city. Just let me walk with you."

I wasn't sure what was going to emerge, but I thought her call of a drastically dramatic essay begged for a drastically boring response. Once her essay was stripped of theatrics, perhaps I would be able to see its "bones" and she could add in more details after it was laid bare. What came back to me was more than a pleasant surprise—it was a beautiful piece of writing. Trinity, it turned out, was an amazingly gifted writer, a talent so masked by her efforts to look interesting that I had never even noticed. She took a day in her life to show her attention to the details of humanity, her keen awareness of her surroundings, and the simple pleasure of walking through an urban area and buying a hot dog. The essay certainly wasn't about an obstacle she had overcome or an achievement she could boast about, and in this instance, a chronology of events was effective because it was infused with literary detail. What emerged allowed for different inferences about Trinity—that she had a heightened sensitivity to her environment, a rich imagination, and a very romantic nature, traits that would certainly help her become a successful actress. Most important, I believe, is that Trinity learned that her everyday self was interesting; she didn't need to embellish anything:

The icy wind of Manhattan winter greets me upon stepping out of the 92nd Street Y and as I walk along my usual route down Lexington Avenue. My breath omits little, foggy clouds that dissipate into the surrounding city atmosphere. I snuggle further into my scarf, regretting not listening to my mother who had told me to wear my fuzzy grey hat with the purple rhinestone flower, the one she had picked up from a boutique de modiste on her latest trip to France. Shivering, I brace myself for the twenty-minute walk back to my apartment.

I see the hot dog stand located on the opposite side of the street. The familiar hot dog man smiles as I approach, revealing his missing tooth and adding a small tilt of his head. He knows that it is time for my after-rehearsal lunch. I order my usual, a hot dog with ketchup, mustard, relish, and no onions. The hot dog man assembles the meal with a repetitive ease, neatly tucking the meat into the bread and layering it with condiments, one ribbon of color at a time. He hands me my meal and gently reminds me that it would be three dollars for the hot dog. "Thank you, sir," I say, as I fish out the crumpled bills tucked away in my jean pocket. I eat the hot dog slowly as I walk, holding it as an emblem of New York City; a symbol of my belonging.

Research

Many colleges ask students why they want to study a particular subject such as, "Why engineering?" "Why pre-med?" or, "How would you solve a world problem?" These are categorical essays that often require students to do research. The research could be watching a film, reading a book, looking for newspaper articles, searching websites, or drawing from something they've learned in school. It's not enough to say, "I want to be able to get a job when I graduate," or, "I've been fascinated with medicine all my life because of the doctors who healed me when I broke my leg." The resolution of world problems is quite difficult to do in just a few hundred words, so these essays can be particularly challenging.

Guiding students to research a very narrow subject matter helps them explain their subject interest and also engages the reader—the student is probably teaching the reader something he or she knows little about. These essays can take a considerable amount of time to research, but once the student has an idea, the writing can go fairly quickly. Writing categorical essays is more familiar to students than narratives. While they have to explain their interests and why they care about an issue, they don't have to justify it at a personal level.

Here are a few excerpts:

· ✳ ·

{ UNIVERSITY OF MICHIGAN }

Describe the unique qualities that attract you to the specific undergraduate College or School to which you are applying. How would that curriculum support your interests?

I recently watched an inspiring documentary presented by ViewChange.org, entitled Unleashing Innovation, which featured engineers from various fields using their skills to create simple solutions for sustainable change in developing communities. Having grown up in Silicon Valley, the hub of technological innovation, and spending many summers in India, I have seen the most extreme circumstances of prosperity as well as poverty. Pursuing an undergraduate degree at Michigan's College of Engineering will allow me to learn skills I see used in Unleashing Innovation and implement them effectively in societies that need them most, such as in India. Michigan's College of Engineering gives undergraduates the ability to combine international policy with engineering, creating a unique interdisciplinary undergraduate experience. Sustainability and public policy are at the forefront of the global agenda. Money is simply not enough anymore, because many communities lack the infrastructure to implement seemingly viable solutions. Pursuing a degree in Michigan's Civil Engineering Department will equip me with skills to help develop sustainable infrastructure in developing countries so they can be self-sufficient in the long run. I am confident that Michigan will enable me to fuse the two distinct worlds that I come from, while also preparing me for the challenge of tackling problems in India and across the globe.

{ ELON UNIVERSITY }

If you were given $10,000 to invest in a project you are passionate about or a business you want to start, what would it be and why? Who would benefit and how would you spend the money? Be specific about the goals you hope to achieve.

If I were given $10,000 to invest in a project I'm passionate about, I would definitely invest it in hearing aids. I could use this $10,000 to start a new hearing aid company that would drastically change the affordability of hearing aids and be dedicated to charitable contributions to the large population of hearing-impaired people.

I've observed two reasons why the need for hearing aids is bound to increase in the coming years. First, the "baby boomer" generation is beginning to reach retirement age, so there will be a large number of senior citizens in the coming years (and seniors are, by far, the largest demographic for hearing aid sales). Secondly, my generation has grown up with iPods, blasting music directly into our ears through the ear buds. I strongly believe that a large number of people who are my age will eventually need hearing aids from sustained ear damage before they even become senior citizens. Technology is so good nowadays that hearing aids are incredibly effective. Most are wireless and some are so small that they aren't even noticeable in the ear! Because of the ease and efficiency of modern hearing aids, I think that a large portion of this growing deafened population will want hearing aids.

This increased demand for hearing aids creates the potential for new markets and high sales, but the high cost of aids leaves low-income people out of the market. High-quality models cost up to $2,000. There are non-profit organizations like the Starkey Foundation that already distribute hearing aids out in third-world countries. I would like to make sure that our low-income citizens in America are served as well.

· ✳ ·

{ UNIVERSITY OF OREGON HONORS COLLEGE }

What international issues matter? Why? If you were an ambassador, how would you try to address them?

One international issue that matters is the future of our natural resources here on Earth, especially our limited freshwater resources. With the population of the Earth already over seven billion people and predicted by the UN to rise to over nine billion by 2050, this issue is becoming increasingly acute with every passing year.

The issue of resource shortages was first widely publicized by English philosopher Thomas Malthus as early as 1798. In An Essay on the Principle of Population, *Malthus stated that population would soon outstrip food production. Malthus argued that when this happened, there would be widespread famine and disease that would in turn check population growth. At the time and for decades afterwards, Malthus' concerns were thought to have been unfounded, as population continued to grow and advances allowed food production to keep pace with it. However, in the past couple of decades, Malthus' predictions have begun to come true, and with the expected population growth over the next century, will become increasingly relevant as our resources begin to run out.*

This problem is so complex that there is no easy way to immediately rectify it and as this is a relatively recent problem there is no international precedent for trying to address it. The ultimate problem is that people who live in dry areas do not have access to enough water and people who live in wet areas often are too wasteful with theirs. However, as ambassador I would try to address this problem by bringing together a global consortium of experts to try to find ways to minimize and eventually find a long-term solution to the problem. I would bring together civil engineers, population demographers, biologists and chemists who specialize in water conservation and procurement and other conservation scientists who would be tasked with finding a solution to this problem.

Popular journalist Malcolm Gladwell, speaking at the majestic Castro Theater in San Francisco in the fall of 2013, was asked by an audience member what surprised him most in his research over the years. Gladwell remarked, "Almost everyone has a really, really great story to tell and are not aware of the fact that they have a great story to tell . . . Insane numbers of people have some fascinating thing in their life, and because it's their life, they have no perspective on it so they don't even realize it's fascinating. And all you have to do is keep the tape recording running long enough and you will find it."

I constantly remind myself of Gladwell's remarks and try to remember to be patient with students who don't enter the writing process with a long list of story ideas. I know the story is there; it just has yet to be found.

CHAPTER 9

THE NEVER-ENDING APPLICATION: BEYOND THE STANDARD ESSAYS

After writing dynamic and categorical essays for the college application, students and their mentors are often surprised to learn that still more writing is asked of students. It seems at times that the amount of information colleges seek is insurmountable. It certainly can feel like that! Beyond the main and supplemental essays that are required for general applicants, colleges increasingly ask for additional information that is not covered elsewhere on the application. After several weeks or months of drafting essays, it's hard to keep up the momentum to answer yet more questions, but colleges may still need to gather additional information they feel is essential to their review. The student needs to muster up the energy to keep on going. At this point, a mentor may be needed less for practical guidance than for sheer support and cheerleading. Or, occasionally, a student needs to seek advice from an expert in a particular field of study. Hopefully by now the student has gotten the hang of the essay process, but these additional questions require the same amount of forethought and attention.

These essays can be identified as the following:

- **THE ELABORATIVE ESSAY:** This part of the application is where a student has the opportunity to provide relevant additional information. The elaborative essay can explain suspensions, poor testing, a change in schools, or the reasons behind a missing high school course. It can also be the appropriate space to explain learning differences such as slow processing, dyslexia, or health conditions (such as a serious concussion or chronic illness) that explain interruptions. Most college applications provide space for students to discuss these special circumstances. These essays tend to be around 150 words, or a short paragraph.

- **THE DIVERSITY FLY-IN ESSAY:** As colleges seek to encourage students from underrepresented backgrounds to visit their campuses, they may ask students to write an essay, separate from the college application, to request funding for the college visit.

- **THE CREATIVE ESSAY:** Required by some departments and schools within a college, creative essays demonstrate creative or analytical writing skills, which will be used to evaluate the fit of the major rather than the fit of the college as a whole.

- **THE INTERNATIONAL STUDENT ESSAY:** This type of essay may be required of students applying to American colleges from other countries. Some questions are required of all international students, while other essays are used for awarding scholarships.

- **THE PERSONAL STATEMENT:** This essay is required of undergraduates applying to colleges in the United Kingdom who use the UCAS (Universities and Colleges Admissions Service) application. This essay is much more similar to what graduate student applicants write in the United States. In these essays, students make a case for their qualifications for a specific course of study.

- **THE QUICK-TAKE:** This is not an essay at all, but several short responses of one or two sentences to questions that colleges may ask in order to give students another opportunity to share their personality, interests, and hobbies in a fun, less serious tone.

The Elaborative Essay

Fortunately, I have found that students who voluntarily explain personal issues fare well. If a student has changed schools three times or has had suspensions, poor test scores, or a few bad grades, it's usually better to do the explaining rather than hope the admission office won't notice or, even more worrisome, draw their own conclusions. It's important for students to keep their responses short and clear—to come across as confident and honest without being unduly apologetic. This is an example of a student who had great grades but felt her SAT scores were an underrepresentation of her academic strengths:

I am a very strong student who does very well in school, but my standardized test scores do not reflect my academic ability. I especially struggled during the SAT with the time limits. I was not able to complete all the questions due to time constraints, but scored mostly correct answers on the questions I did complete. I am confident I'll be successful in the academic programs at Madison.

For many students, one of the great fears of applying to college is disclosing something about themselves that they are not proud of, or worrying that a college might deny them access because of school disruptions, periods in residential treatment, physical or other disabilities, or mental health challenges.

While it is not legally required for students to disclose physical or mental disabilities, for students whose academic record shows periods of poor performance or disruption, a carefully crafted essay can be of great benefit.

Although it's not necessary, in order to go above and beyond a clear and simple explanation, some students may choose to write a dynamic essay rather than an elaborative essay to talk about experiences going through residential treatment. They may feel their story aligns well with narrative prompts and are comfortable telling "their story."

I have worked with many teens who have lived through dark times. Students who have had extensive therapy are often much easier to mentor because they have had a lot of mentoring already and have come to understand their own psychology. They may feel very comfortable writing a long essay about their journey back to wellness.

Here are examples of two students who chose to elaborate on their educational history and emotional health through a dynamic essay. They are what I refer to as "Long Elaborations."

Below is Veronica's Common Application essay. It was written while she was still in residential treatment, but she expressed optimism about her future and her ability to handle the rigor of college life.

Discuss an accomplishment or event, formal or informal, that marked your transition from childhood to adulthood within your culture, community, or family.

It was so much more than a performance. It was a reflection of all the progress I have made. The biggest event at North Star Academy, and I was singing at it. I was singing at the North Star Alumni Gala where current girls and their families and graduated girls and their families come back to celebrate.

That solo performance among my peers marked my transition from childhood to adulthood because I performed with the confidence of a young adult.

I remember looking at my parents sitting in the audience when I was singing the lyrics: "When you believe, somehow you will. You will when you believe." All our eyes were watering because they saw it too; I had grown into a happier and more mature person.

In my heart I knew I wanted to audition for this gala performance, but I was nervous.

On the outside, I am a social butterfly, but on the inside I'm a little more reserved. I was always nervous and embarrassed about my singing. I was good, but my confidence was low. I performed a lot when I was younger, but had a hiatus during sophomore and junior year because of personal struggles. In high school I wanted to put myself out there, but didn't have the confidence to do so. I thought to myself, "Veronica, if you don't put yourself out there, how will you ever know what you can do?" So I auditioned. I am so happy I did.

In February I moved to Utah. I needed a change. I wasn't myself. I left Seattle angry, sad, and hopeless. This was a hard decision to leave my school in Seattle and move out of state. I have been living in a boarding school for about eight months now and I have had many opportunities to regain my confidence in many areas. Throughout this move to a new school and a temporary home, music has been a constant. That is how I know it is so important in my life.

I was introduced to jazz and theatre at the age of six. It absorbed my whole family. My parents are actors and musicians so they would be a part of our school musicals and take us to shows. At the age of seven, I joined a jazz-performing group in Seattle. We were called the JazzKids. We performed anywhere from shopping malls to symphony halls. I consider myself very much of an old soul. I believe that classic songs are timeless.

From classic jazz standards by Miles Davis, Frank Sinatra, Etta James, Ella Fitzgerald, and Sarah Vaughn to soul masters like Otis Redding and Aretha Franklin to contemporary artists such as Amy Winehouse, these people inspire me. I admire these artists specifically because I aspire to perform music in their genre. I have a big imagination and music takes me everywhere. I picture myself in Carnegie Hall or at Lincoln Center with a trio of bass, piano, and drums singing a blues rendition of "Black Coffee."

At a very young age I knew I wanted to be a performer. During high school I lost my motivation because of my fears and uncertainty about my esteem, but at North Star I got my passion back. This is what I am supposed to do. This is what makes me happy.

Once the concert was over I was overwhelmed with an array of emotions: ecstatic, proud, and supported.

I will never forget the feeling I had walking off of the stage and having my friends and family give me hugs. All of my insecurities went away. I felt on top of the world like I can conquer anything: school, struggles, relationships, and life.

Another student took a gap year after attending a residential treatment program. Being a little bit older, and with the ability to be retrospective about her experiences, she wrote a long elaborative essay that demonstrated her growth since graduating from high school.

Some students have a background or story that is so central to their identity that they believe their application would be incomplete without it. If this sounds like you, then please share your story.

For eight years I struggled with an eating disorder that kept me firmly docked in my comfort zone. It may seem imprudent to reveal such a "weakness." However, exposing my vulnerabilities is a risk I am willing to take because behind all the data that you'll see in my file, stands a sincere, strong woman. I would never deny my past struggles because it reveals my resiliency. When I graduated from my residential treatment program, my teacher gave me this quote, "A ship is safe in harbor, but that's not what ships are for." I think about this a lot, because it gives me the confidence to share this story.

One year ago, I was taking a full course load and thinking about college applications just like everyone else. For me, anything other than doing what was expected was out of the question, for the expected is the predictable, and I liked living in that cozy space of always knowing what my future would hold. I did not want to risk disappointing others, so I quietly and unwaveringly played by the rules.

I was a perfectly high-functioning person in my eating disorder; it would have been hard for anyone to guess that on the inside I was crumbling under the weight of my own self-doubt, criticism, and discouragement. I constantly prioritized what I thought other people wanted to see from me, and I made sure to never rock the boat, to always fly under the radar. I could easily have stayed in high school and no one would have known my secret. But, as I know now, a truly meaningful and worthwhile life doesn't begin until you choose to boldly knock down those walls that we all build around ourselves.

I chose to suspend my senior year to focus on my health. I was at a residential treatment center figuring out who I am, learning how to tolerate distress, ask for help, strengthening my unique voice, and inspiring and being inspired by others who understood my struggles. With each small risk I took, from letting myself cry in front of near strangers to learning how to gallop on a horse, to voicing my unpopular opinion about a community concern, I grew.

Since this experience, I've graduated from high school with the rest of my class and landed two jobs that challenge me to interact with people daily. I'm taking community college courses and mastering the art of living in an apartment with a roommate. The future looks promising in terms of sustaining my voyage. My goals include studying Spanish in Argentina, skiing in Patagonia, running my first 5K, and starting a draft of an inspirational novel for adolescents. I am so thankful to finally be truly living, not just existing. Perfection and security, though glorified by society, are boring; it's the rocking of the boat that makes life exciting. My days of feeling safe in harbor are over because this ship is more than ready to steer her course through life!

This essay boldly begins with the student's identification with an eating disorder. The student had spent time in a treatment program where she completed high school. Her academic record would be without context if she didn't make this disclosure. She wrote an honest and hopeful essay about where she had been and her optimism for the future, sharing both vulnerability and strength of character.

The Diversity Fly-In Essay

Underrepresented, low-income students may not have the means to fly across the country visiting campuses. Many colleges have "fly-in" programs that fund airfare, ground transportation, and meals for prospective students who demonstrate strong academics as well as motivation to be a bit of a trailblazer, while being willing to attend a college that might be slowly building a diverse community. Usually these grants are awarded to students who submit an essay along with a transcript. Occasionally, a letter of recommendation is also required, even though the student has not yet applied to the college.

{ Draft 1 }

Why is diversity important to you?

Diversity is not only what makes us different, diversity is what all humans have in common. It is the middle ground where we can all empathize and relate to one another. Diversity is the future; different ways of thinking allow innovative ideas that can change how we perceive and reason. Diversity forces people to open their minds and accept that all people are different, but in a setting like a university, it is clear that all are equal; all of those students were chosen to be a perfect fit for the specific school, meaning they all have that in common and they all have that capacity to be successful.

Marisol's initial approach to this essay was to try to discern what diversity meant to the university rather than her own personal experience with diversity. She wanted to appear politically correct and felt she was being asked a question for which there was only one answer. She wrote what she thought the university wanted to hear and there was nothing in the first draft about her personal experience as a Mexican-American student whose first language was Spanish. After Marisol showed me her first draft, I asked her to write specifically about her own classroom experience. The result was a far better essay and a round-trip ticket to the East Coast.

Sitting in my AP Spanish class, my teacher asks me once again if I am familiar with yet another Mexican normality, or classic novel or popular soap opera. I look around the room and notice everyone stares at me, curious to know what the only Mexican in the classroom has to say about our topic of conversation. What is the Mexican perspective on Gabriel García Márquez? Where do Mexicans stand on the obesity issue in the Americas? I often feel uncomfortable, embarrassed even, that I am expected to represent a whole ethnicity in some classroom situations. Arbor High School seems to be very diverse, and although my school has what I feel is a sufficient Latino population—25 percent—there seems to be an invisible line that separates all ethnic groups at school. There are almost no other Latino students enrolled in AP classes and I am often the only Latina in my class. I wish my classmates represented the diversity in my school. Diversity in the classroom is important to me because I don't want to be singled out because of my race. Diversity is important to me because I don't want to be only classified by a race; I want to be known for my abilities, my strengths and my personality. I want to use my heritage and background to offer a different point of view, but I don't want to be the sole representative of my culture for my peers. I'm the odd one out in my AP classes now—I'd like to go to your university where the mission is to unite students of all backgrounds so that everyone feels part of an inclusive environment.

THE CREATIVE ESSAY

The creative essay is common for students applying to specialized and usually highly selective programs, such as film, creative writing, marketing, and fine or performing arts. Applicants are asked to demonstrate a level of maturity and experience in their field of study beyond what would be typical of most high school students. They will often have completed internships, work experience, coursework, or summer programs that provide them with the experience to respond to these questions.

These specific assignments may require additional help from someone other than the mentor. Experts in the fields that students wish to study may be in the best position to offer specialized guidance on this piece of the application.

In no more than two (2) pages, describe a public relations or advertising campaign that you found particularly effective or offensive. Examine the overall

goal or message of the campaign, how that message was delivered, and if you feel the campaign was successful. You may choose to examine a campaign you have organized or in which you were a participant.

Living in the Bay Area, people assume that I live by the Pacific Ocean. While geographically this may be true much more pronounced is the sea of black and orange that I am surrounded by, especially in the month of October. The excitement that the San Francisco Giants create is evident throughout the Bay, and whether or not you follow the team, the energy that the fans generate is contagious.

"Together We're Giant" has been one of the Giants' main advertising campaigns beginning spring of 2011. Through their series of commercials, YouTube videos, Facebook page, Twitter, etc. "Together We're Giant" has been the baseball team's anthem for the past season. This campaign is highly effective for many reasons; it engages the targeted audience, it creates a sense of unity, and is accessible to a wide demographic.

The Giants produced a series of short thirty-second commercials that each end with the slogan, "Together We're Giant." These commercials strive to make the viewer feel as though he/she is a part of the team. Each clip uses a real player from the team, such as Matt Cain, Buster Posey, or Pablo Sandoval, as well as using real Giants fans. The commercials create a reciprocal feeling; the fans cheer for the Giants and the Giants players play their best for the fans. This sense of unity is a driving force behind this campaign and is achieved in many ways. Throughout the videos there are split screens showing the fans and the player coming together with a plus sign in the middle. In one video, Buster Posey is shown swinging at a ball but becomes replaced by a montage of fans also hitting the ball creating the illusion that the fans became Buster. Likewise, in another ad where Ryan Vogelsong is featured the narrator reminds the viewer that we all "see ourselves in an all-star like Ryan." The clips also utilize more subtle ways to make their audience feel like part of the team by choosing diction that are synonyms for "together" like "combined," for example. In one video, the word "plus" is used ten times in thirty seconds.

In addition to fostering a sense of unity, the campaign reaches out to a wide variety of fans. Different groups of fans are presented in the videos, displaying the diversity of the fan base. One commercial features a woman from Pablo Sandoval's hometown in Venezuela, a group of little girls, a season ticket holder from 1972, and a family. Presenting many different types of fans that come out to Giants games allows the viewers to potentially see themselves in the commercial.

The "Together We're Giant" campaign is highly successful which shows in the team's consecutive sold-out games. Not only does the campaign help sell tickets, but it also has helped to create a large loyal fan base, evident in the fact that 10,000 fans braced the cold to watch their team win the World Series on a screen at the San Franicsco Civic Center.

INTERNATIONAL STUDENT ESSAYS

With an increasing number of students applying to American universities from abroad, some colleges have specific questions they wish them to address. The findings in a 2013 report of the Commission on International Student Recruitment to the National Association for College Admissions Counseling (NACAC) noted that "globalization, enhanced technology, and increased mobility have increased both the demand and supply for international education." Simultaneously, public funding at state schools has declined in recent years, and international students, who generally pay higher tuition fees, have become part of strategic recruitment plans across the country. At the University of California, for example, 22,546 international students applied for admission to the entering class of 2014.

International students may find it challenging to write an essay in their non-native language and need to be sure their English grammar is consistent with their TOEFL or IELTS score and other indicators of English proficiency as evidenced from college entrance exams and coursework. An overly edited, perfectly grammatically correct essay could look questionable if written by a student whose TOEFL score indicates limited English proficiency.

For international students, it *is* okay for their "accent" to come through. Students who do not speak American English, such as Australian or British students, might use spelling, grammatical structures, and vocabulary that an American student wouldn't typically use. As long as the essay is clear, the lexicon and syntax of the student should be natural to them.

The following is an excerpt from an essay written by an Australian student:

Being elected by the popular vote of the Headmaster, Deputy Headmaster, Reverend, and boys of the school is a very humbling experience that provided a very coveted opportunity to express my individualism as a leader of the school. My contributions as a member of such an elite task force levied the importance of making a positive impact upon the school this year whilst displaying my characteristics and abilities as a leader. I strive to be a person that individuals of society can look up to and enjoy the company of. In attaining this position, I did not see myself as solely a leader, but as a representative of the moralistic and cultural paradigms of my community, whilst redressing any retrospective views or problems that we face as students.

While most colleges don't have special application requirements for international students beyond proof of English competency, a small number of colleges have added essays specifically for international students.

Discuss a significant issue in your home country about which you are passionate and describe how you would use the education you obtain at the American University, Washington DC, to creative positive civic and social change once you return home. (250 words max)

Technology makes our lives easier, with the broad circulation of iPhones, tablets, and computers. But once technology is improperly disposed of, it has an unforgiving effect on the well-being of others. There is not enough awareness about the problems with e-waste. I am from Chandigarh, India where I see rag pickers sift through this e-waste in order to recycle the valuable parts that can be used again. The health effects from poisonous components of e-waste like lead and chromium are visible from a distance, due to toxic elements inside the components. Because of the large labor force available in India and the increasing amount of electronic goods, the e-waste industry is booming. The effort made to recycle certain material is definitely beneficial, but the impact on human health outweighs any material gain from this effort.

It matters to me that we uphold the principle of accountability, and that regions like Chandigarh, India are not polluted by toxic waste from broken technology. I know that a degree in Public Health from American will prepare me to impact this public health issue in my community in India. I am especially interested in developing research and analytical skills that will enable me to plan and execute a solution to this ongoing health issue by working to provide incentives for safe recycling programs while simultaneously educating rag pickers about the dangers of their work and helping communities find other means of employment for the poorest citizens.

ESSAYS FOR AMERICAN STUDENTS APPLYING TO UNIVERSITIES IN THE UNITED KINGDOM

Increasingly, universities abroad are reaching out to American students for much the same reasons American universities seek international students. American students add to the diversity on campus and pay higher tuition than domestic students. The United Kingdom uses a system similar to the American Common Application. Their universal application is called the UCAS (Universities and Colleges Admissions Service). Applicants can apply to a maximum of five universities through this single application and must write just one personal statement that each university will receive. In the United Kingdom, students apply directly to a particular course of study, similar to what we call a major in the United States. Instead of writing a dynamic essay, applicants using the UCAS write a personal statement that is read by the teaching faculty of the course of study rather than by an admission committee. It is the faculty that will determine which students will be admitted, similar to how graduate school admission is conducted in the United States. Just like the Common Application, the UCAS essays are not customized for specific campuses. A personal statement is an opportunity for a student to make the case that they are qualified and suitable for the course of study they have chosen. UCAS asks why the subject is of interest to the student, what the student's goals are on completion of the course of study, and what preparation the student has for the course of study (which can include work experience, secondary school courses, leadership, or activities that are related to the course of study). The personal statement is limited to 4,000 characters, or about forty-seven lines of text including spaces and blank lines on the online form. American students need to choose a course of study knowing that almost all of their coursework toward their degree will be in a single subject area.

Here is an example of a personal statement for the UCAS:

I want to study International Relations in the United Kingdom where I can experience another culture and gain first-hand knowledge of England's government. I wish to be a Public Diplomacy Officer for the United States Foreign Service.

An International Relations course will prepare me for this career in many ways. The program will provide me with knowledge of state foreign policies and regional histories of international engagement. But more importantly, an International Relations course will illuminate me to the philosophy that explains greater trends in world diplomacy.

I have been an active participant in my school's Model United Nations Club as an officer, and helped organize my club's participation in conferences at several universities. I was a delegate in conferences at Stanford, Duke, and Tufts University. At Stanford, I represented Greece in the North Atlantic Treaty Organization, and was awarded the distinction of "Best Delegate" at the end of the conference. Participating in Model United Nations has given me a solid introduction to the study of international relations, as well as affirming my passion for world diplomacy.

I believe my conversational fluency in Spanish will be an asset to me as a diplomat. I have studied Spanish in school for five years and participated in a two-week immersion course in Guatemala when I was in the seventh grade. In my sophomore year of high school, I traveled to Spain and lived with a Spanish family for a month.

I also I have a comprehensive understanding of United State's history, the function of its government, and its foreign policy after taking Advanced Placement classes in American History, American Government and Politics, and Economics. Besides academic courses, I have participated in Harvard Model Congress, an intellectual educational simulation of the U.S. government where I held roles as a Supreme Court Justice, and Secretary of Labor in the Presidential Cabinet at national conferences.

I am most proud of my writing skills, which I'm sure will allow me to write research papers of the highest quality. I have been a writer and editor for my national-award-winning school newspaper. I also write a monthly opinion column in our local city newspaper, in which I expose exigent issues. Last year, I won a national award for high school journalists.

I sincerely wish for the opportunity to study International Relations in the UK; I know it is the perfect path for me.

QUICK TAKES

And finally, some colleges ask for "quick takes"—a maximum of one or two sentences that the student is supposed to respond to like an elevator pitch. Of course, students put as much thought into these "quick takes" as they do into longer essays. Encapsulating personal information in two sentences or less is much harder that it seems.

Here's an example of a student who was able to communicate the warmth of his character through this exercise:

Please answer the following statements in no more than two sentences (250 characters):

What would you consider to be your greatest accomplishment?

My greatest accomplishment was when I created my own flag football league. Unable to discover a quality recreational flag football league in my area, I gathered every teenager I knew and created the "BFL" with over forty players with jerseys, team names, referees and coaches.

What is the best piece of advice you have received?

Ever since I was a little kid, my grandfather has constantly reminded me, "It pays to be nice." I have found one can never be disliked if one takes every opportunity given to do something nice for someone, whether it's a friendly "good morning" when passing a stranger on my walk to school or helping an underclassman with homework.

What would you do with a free afternoon tomorrow?

What many people do not know about me is I love to spend my free time in the kitchen. I love taking a boring soup and making it pop with an array of spices and herbs or taking a whole chicken and turning it into a dish my whole family will love.

In the year 2030 your name and picture appear in the news. What is the headline?

The headline would read, 'The Seattle Times' own Marshall Plaat honored at sports writing event." I have had a splendid time covering sports for my high school's newspaper and see myself continuing to share my passion for sports writing in the future.

THE SECRET READER

Once a student has completed and is satisfied with all their essays, I send them off to be read by a "secret reader." The secret reader is given the essay only with the essay question, the list of colleges that will receive this essay, and the student's academic profile. Secret readers don't edit the essay, but report back to me on what they have inferred about the student. Earlier in this book, the concept of inferences and the college essay was explored. Ultimately, an essay is successful if the reader infers what the writer intended. If the secret reader's impressions are synonymous with how I believe the student wants to be represented, then the essay is a success. If the reader's interpretation of the student is different from how the student wants to be perceived, the student is provided with that feedback and we take a look together to see how the reader inferred something that was unintended by the writer. The students know that secret readers will provide feedback and they look forward to that informal report. My small group of secret readers provides an essential service to the end goal of the Better Essay.

CHAPTER 10

THE BETTER ESSAY
IN ACTION

This chapter illustrates the cycle of mentorship by providing a first draft, the mentor's comments, and a student's final draft. I chose these essays because they clearly illustrate how "editing without a pen" and providing a student with just a few very specific questions or comments can really turn an essay into something quite exceptional.

{ OREN—DRAFT 1 }

Describe a setting in which you have collaborated or interacted with people whose experiences and/or beliefs differ from yours. Address your initial feelings, and how those feelings were or were not changed by this experience.

Growing up in the Bay Area has given me opportunities to see the lives of others outside of my own community. Living in my small neighborhood I never really saw much diversity, but when I first traveled to Salinas, just outside of the Bay Area for a baseball tournament, I was in shock. Playing baseball I noticed the smaller houses, the graffiti in the streets, and lots of people doing backbreaking work in the fields. After the trip I asked my dad who these people were and what were they doing. He responded by saying they were migrant farmers and they were picking the food we eat. After learning a little more about the topic I could not believe the things going on just an hour away from where I live. It was not until high school that I was given the opportunity to really help out the people of Salinas. My school offered an "Immersion" program designed to immerse ourselves with the people we worked. It was a two-week program where we worked, served and lived with some of the migrant farmers in the Salinas area. For the first time in my life, I experienced the hardships these people faced their entire lives. I got to experience what it was like to work all day in the fields, weeding and harvesting crops. It gave me a new respect and a new *understanding of what the migrant farmers have to work through. My eight-person group was tired, sore, and overheated at the end of a long day, but we realized that we saved the farmers a few backbreaking weeks in the fields. The "immersion" challenged me in another way by allowing us to live on $50 a day, following what a migrant family might have to live on in a day. Coming from my well-off family, going to the supermarket was never a challenge; I could just buy whatever food I wanted. The budget challenged myself and the group to work together to create meals that kept us under budget and meals that everyone would enjoy. After the program I can now use the tools I learned shopping to help lower my family's budget. The most important part of the program was working with the children of the migrant farmers. We were in charge of running a camp for them in a field nearby their residence. The income levels of the migrant families and my own showed up the most at the kid's camp. I kept on thinking about the camps I went to, where we had all the equipment we needed to do hundreds of different activities, but I soon realized that at the camp it was going to be different. I used whatever we had to start a soccer game. We brought a soccer ball but used old plywood as goals. The camp allowed me to see what other kids were suffering through and through the power of games we could all enjoy some friendly competition.*

COMMENTS:

- Decide to make the emphasis on an ethical dilemma rather than an experience.
- Identify what the ethical dilemma is.
- Focus on the plight of the migrant worker—give a name to someone you met.
- Remove the "rich" versus "poor" focus.
- Do research on the farm.
- Read an article published by Stanford on the benefits of organic food to consumers and workers.

{ OREN—FINAL DRAFT }

Before my summer of junior year, I had never really been a person to think about who grows my food or where that food comes from, but as the school service trip approached, I was about to find myself in a whole new world. The trip was a two-week

"Immersion" program to Salinas in California's Central Valley where my group and I would live alongside the migrant farmers. While there, I learned about the migrant farmers' lifestyle and their working conditions. I worked with Geronimo who had just recently been given the opportunity to start his own small farm. This land was given to him along with the knowledge of how to start an organic farm by a non-profit, ALBA Farms. After three hours of grueling, backbreaking work on the fields with Geronimo, I soon understood the struggles of farming organically without using pesticides. After weeding three rows of cauliflower, my fingers were cut and bleeding, two blisters beginning to form on the palm of my right hand. I mustered up the courage to ask Geronimo the reasons for starting an organic farm. He talked about the obvious reasons: it was better for the land, better for the people eating the food, but his biggest reason was to protect his health from pesticides so he could take care of his three sons. As a migrant, he is unable to get quality medical care. As part of our experience, we had to buy the food for my group of ten students on just $50 per day. We were given that money to simulate what the average migrant farmer will need to feed their families. Walking through the Smart & Final was an experience that I will never forget. The store seemed so much bigger. With the limited budget, finding food to feed ten people seemed almost impossible. Each group member made their case for meals and we quickly realized that our diets were going to consist of chicken, sausage, and pasta and the entire group had to like the food. We often resorted to instant oatmeal and Cheerios. With $15 left in the budget, we considered buying some healthy fruits and vegetables. Then, I began to understand the problems with buying cheap healthy food. I was looking for some healthy strawberries that could be enjoyed by everyone and I found a small package that was locally grown. I realized that they were not organic and we were working on organic farms. I found the ALBA farms organically grown brand that Geronimo sells to and they were $2 more. In the produce section, I was faced with the ethical dilemma of whether I should buy the cheaper, non-organic food, or the more expensive organically grown produce by local farms. I made the choice of buying the cheapest fruit. Now, I've read that Stanford University's study found that organic food is not healthier than non-organic food. But is the health of the migrant worker worth the $2 extra I would have paid?

I love how this essay evolved from a very typical description of a service trip to an essay that illustrates the ethical lessons learned from the trip. His take-away was unexpected. He learned much more than the living conditions of migrant workers—he learned that his very actions as a consumer of produce had a direct impact on the lives of the workers.

{ MARIANNA—DRAFT 1 }

_____

Describe a character in fiction, a historical figure, or a creative work (as in art, music, science, etc.) that has had an influence on you, and explain that influence.

ODC/Dance, a modern dance company in San Francisco, has a piece in its repertoire titled "24 Exposures" choreographed by Brenda Way. Because I have trained as a dancer at the ODC School, I have been able to observe company rehearsals and performances. As a result, I have been fortunate enough to see "24 Exposures" multiple times and become familiar with Way's other works as well as with her artistic process. "24 Exposures," set to music by Yo-Yo Ma and Mark O'Connor, was intended to explore the evolution of modern dance over time. The piece begins with pedestrian movement, shifts into contemporary ballet, and ends with a fusion of both extreme styles.

This piece always makes me cry.

As an artist, I appreciate both the aesthetics of a movement piece as well as the message that the piece sends whether it is intentional or inadvertent. Although "24 Exposures" was not intended to have any sort of ethical lesson, watching this piece over and over again has allowed me to pull out lessons for myself that influence my own work as a dancer and choreographer in profound ways.

First, I have found that movement does not need to be visually complicated or technically challenging in order for it to be beautiful. In fact, the simplest movement, a gesture, is often what gives a movement phrase accessibility and power. In "24 Exposures," there is one point where only two dancers are left onstage, a man and a woman, and they begin an adagio duet. The woman falls, and the man catches her by the neck and rocks her head back and forth like a baby. It does not take years of training in a dance studio for dancers to be able to create that moment; however, that is always the moment where I burst into tears. That simple movement, the rocking, reminds me of how whenever I fall or whenever I feel defeated, I turn to my loved ones for comfort and support. That simple movement reminds me of what the premise of love really is: providing support so that one can rise up on their own and triumph over obstacles.

For the last three years, I have been a company member in the ODC/Dance's teen modern dance company: The ODC Dance Jam. While working with guest choreographers, I am constantly asked to provide movement sequences to incorporate into the piece. Whether the choreographer wants a fast, athletic phrase or a slow, flowing phrase, I always make sure to add at least one isolated, simple movement. Whether it is the flick of a wrist or the bowing of the head, I know that the incorporation of that move will be the key ingredient to make the sequence accessible and powerful to an audience.

COMMENTS:

- Have you choreographed anything? If so, include it.

- Start the essay with an emphasis on yourself and not the dance company.

- Circle back to "24 Exposures" at the end.

{ MARIANNA—FINAL DRAFT }

"24 Exposures," a piece in the ODC/Dance repertoire, greatly influences my work as a student choreographer.

This piece, choreographed by ODC/Dance's Artistic Director Brenda Way, is intended to explore the evolution of modern dance over time. It begins with postmodern movement, shifts into contemporary ballet, and ends with a fusion of both styles. As a student dancer and choreographer at the ODC Dance School, I have had the opportunity to observe and study "24 Exposures," both in rehearsal and in performance, over several years. As a result, I have been able to extract lessons from the piece that influence my own work.

Movement does not need to be visually complicated or technically challenging in order for it to be beautiful. In fact, the simplest movement, a gesture, can captivate the audience in ways that other movements cannot. Because it is isolated, a gesture allows the audience to focus on that singular movement. In "24 Exposures," there are a few minutes in the second section where only two dancers are left onstage, a man and a woman. They begin an adagio duet. The woman falls, and the man catches her by the neck and rocks her head back and forth like a baby. That is always the moment that touches me the most. That effortless movement, the rocking, reminds me of how whenever I fall or whenever I feel defeated, I turn to my loved ones for comfort and support.

I realized that the rocking movement is so powerful because of its placement. It is embedded in a long, visually and technically complex sequence that gives the audience a greater appreciation of its simplicity.

I am experimenting with that technique of embedding isolated movements into complex sequences. At the end of a section of a piece that I am currently creating, a female dancer performs a fierce, almost hysterical, movement phrase in the center of the stage without traveling. I fix the spotlight on her. The dancer suddenly stops and faces the audience. I exchange the music with a pre-recorded rhythmic stomping of the foot. The dancer does nothing except hold up her hand and lightly flick it to the beat of the stomping. The light fades into darkness, and the stomping continues for a few seconds before the next section begins.

This visual sequence expresses a rite of passage. The repeating gesture resembles the ticking of a clock, as if time is passing, and, in that time, the girl is growing. The dancer's stillness occurs upon realizing that the audience is witnessing her outburst. She displays the beginning of her maturity into young adulthood.

I attend as many professional dance performances as I possibly can. In doing so, I continue to learn new techniques for creating an aesthetically beautiful and intellectually stimulating piece. It is my goal to one day create a piece as memorable as "24 Exposures."

With little direction, Marianna took the opportunity to walk the reader through her own creation of a dance piece, applying her own creative process into what she learned from watching the work of choreographer Brenda Way. In this essay, the focus is more on Marianna and how she is capable of not only understanding dance, but also creating it.

Tell us about a personal quality, talent, accomplishment, contribution or experience that is important to you. What about this quality or accomplishment makes you proud and how does it relate to the person you are?

Confusion and disbelief spread over the faces of onlookers. Tourists stared, contemplating the reasons why my mother and I, and thousands of other people, are wearing wetsuits and Speedos while walking through downtown San Francisco at 7 o'clock on a Sunday morning. My mother introduced me to open water swimming when I was fifteen years old. The mental and physical challenge keeps me. The adventures of Lynne Cox, an open water swimmer and author of books on her adventures, was a great inspiration to me.

The ferry ride out to Alcatraz Island is stressful, yet even on a boat of competitors there is a feeling of camaraderie. Glancing outside, I watch two coast guard boats positioning themselves, a few jet skis, and hundreds of kayakers scattered throughout the Bay, all present to rescue any swimmers that run into trouble. I know I'm prepared, because I've been training. Once the ferries are aligned with Alcatraz, there is a dramatized countdown and we are given the order to jump. It is an order; race officials have a short window, less than two minutes, to get over 500 swimmers off each boat. As soon as my body hits the cold water, the mammalian diving reflex kicks in, and my heart rate slows in order to conserve energy.

Instinctively I begin swimming quickly, looking to pull ahead of the swimmers around me. The long distance from Alcatraz Island back to San Francisco requires me to conserve as much energy as possible and so as not to burn out. My stroke is long and begins down in my hips, trying not to move the water itself, but to use the water as resistance with which to pull on and glide through.

Time passes and the coastline still seems impossibly far away. I estimate we have been in the water for thirty minutes. I am still doing breast stroke and we are only half way there. In previous swims I usually finish in around thirty minutes, usually placing in my age group. This swim is different, and as time passes I begin to feel my muscles freezing up.

The mental game begins; the water in the bay is unsanitary to say the least; I don't mind the salt—it's the taste of the gasoline in the water that I despise. My skin stings from the icy water, my stomach hurts from ingesting too much of it. The swells around me are massive, undulating walls of water that block any sight of other swimmers. As we approach the finish, the city grows larger. Time speeds up, events occur in snapshots. I can see them now, cheering. Up on the beach towards the finish line, my legs are clumsy as they relearn to walk. The sound is deafening.

COMMENTS:

- Too top heavy in the description of the race start.

- Did you swim with a friend or with a team?

- Elaborate on the reference to the open water swimmer or remove as it doesn't seem to relate to your story on this day.

- Did anyone watch your race?

{ STEPHEN—FINAL DRAFT }

I know I'm prepared. I've been waking up at 5 in the morning to swim in the Bay, training to swim in open water races from the prison on Alcatraz Island to the shores of San Francisco. My mother gives me something new to worry about—today she's swimming with me. My goal wasn't to end up on the podium this time, but to help my mom, at age fifty-four, complete this swim safely.

A week before the race I had offered to "sight" for her, and guide her in so that she could simply follow me and not have to worry about currents or watching landmarks. Although this was my fifth Alcatraz swim, this was my first with my mom.

A horn blows and over 1,000 swimmers begin jumping ten feet from Alcatraz into the water. I take my mom's hand and lead her near the front of the pack; together we jump in. As soon as my body hits the cold water, the mammalian diving reflex kicks in, and my heart rate slows in order to conserve energy.

Instinctively I begin swimming quickly, looking to pull ahead of the swimmers around me. After ten strokes I look back, remembering my mom. Seeing her far behind me, I swim backwards. "You are doing great! Breathe!" I shout over the waves. She swims slowly. I swim breaststroke next to her, keeping an eye on the coastline.

Every few strokes I give a thumbs up and shout words of encouragement. The coast-line still seems impossibly far away. I estimate we have been in the water for thirty minutes. I am still doing breaststroke and we are only half way there. In previous swims I usually finish in around thirty minutes. This swim is different, and as time passes I begin to feel my muscles freezing up.

The mental game begins. The water in the bay is unsanitary to say the least; I don't mind the salt—it's the taste of the gasoline in the water that I despise. My skin stings from the icy water, my stomach hurts from ingesting too much of it. I focus on the present and try to stay positive, smiling at my mom, taking breaks to let her rest every 300 meters or so.

As we approach the finish, the city grows larger. Time speeds up, events occur in snapshots. I slow to make sure my mom and I finish together. My feet find solid ground, stumbling to gain footing. Reaching over, I help my mom stand. My mother and I hug and step across the finish line with our arms around each other. My dad took a photo. This experience was far more rewarding than any of the first- or second-place medals that I had received in previous races. I felt a great sense of accomplishment in helping my mother achieve this remarkable test of physical and mental determination. And thousands of tourists standing on the shore watching for us applauded too.

When Stephen mentioned that his mother swam with him, the focus and intrigue of the entire essay turned. His list of accomplishments on his college application had already revealed his success as an open water champion, but swimming with his mother put a whole new spin on Stephen. His parents are divorced, information the college knew from other parts of his application. Including the father in the story, who waited on the shore for Stephen and his mother, added a glimpse into the relationships within his family. Stephen's parents were able to put aside their differences to support their son— providing insight into where this student finds confidence.

{ TYLER—DRAFT 1 }

Tell us about a personal quality, talent, accomplishment, contribution or experience that is important to you. What about this quality or accomplishment makes you proud and how does it relate to the person you are?

There was a jubilant yell in front of the hotel as our team found out that we made finals. The atmosphere was rejuvenated and lively and I felt relieved as we headed into the final round of RoboSub 16, where teams built autonomous submarines that complete underwater tasks. My emotion and nostalgia came from thinking how far I came since I started my passion of robotics, the energy I had invested in this club's development, and the satisfaction of all this work paying off. The team itself was the most important factor, as I remembered as their input, ideas, spirit, and determination made this memorable victory possible. This team built up my capabilities and I had a profound effect on my peers likewise. We came here as a team, we qualified as a team, and now that we had come this far, it was time to put the icing on the cake and to finish the competition with a bang.

The passion staring at a computer screen for hours, hand sawing metal, and accidentally breathing solder fumes was an activity that I grew interested in over time. The environment where I grew up in had a large affect on this hobby. The Silicon Valley was bustling in technology companies. From Roombas, robot vacuums, to Photoshop, the influence of technology was everywhere. From technology came robotics. My dad used to frequently take me to a robotics convention in San Jose, where they displayed robots made from Legos, to humanoids. The possibilities presented in these conventions fascinated me. This led to my interest in Lego Mindstorms robotics in middle school, where my interests in the field picked up. Of course, since half my team had Lego robotics at home we essentially won all the intra-school competitions. We were the giants then. But the tables had turned as we came into this college competition, as now we were the underdogs. So here is where the function of teamwork truly shined.

To make it to this moment, a final team in this collegiate competition, software members like me had to contribute much more than just writing code. Each member of the team was delegated a few responsibilities to accommodate the multitude of tasks that needed attention. For example, I had to extend our reach for grants and sponsors, to educate new members interested in programming, to spend long hours during the school year and almost every day of summer with the team in someone's garage to build on our progress. These extra efforts made our position much more rewarding. Working with dedicated members on these tasks, I came to realize the value of determination, cooperation, and the synergistic effect when these characteristics are met.

All these experiences now came full circle as I was heading to the pool with the sub to test new software fixes for the final event. At this point we were already overwhelmed by the fact that we made it to the final rounds and just wanted to fix any possible problems. Members started to mobilize and working on different tasks, even if the job was out of their specific field. Seeing this and all that we had been through together, I was proud to work with and represent this dedicated and still developing team. It is these experiences that made we wonder what can be achieved with persistence in my passions, but also with a relation between those who reflect my interests.

COMMENTS:

- How exactly did you find out you made the finals?

- Give your team and your robot a name.

- Tell us what your robot does.

{ TYLER—FINAL DRAFT }

There was a jubilant yell in front of the hotel in Santa Monica as our team, JKBotz, got the tweet that we made RoboSub 16 finals—a collegiate robotics competition. Our autonomous submarine, we named "Barracuda," was going to complete underwater tasks in a final event in the competition pool. Barracuda was about three feet long and weighed ninety pounds. My contribution was writing code so that Barracuda could pass through an underwater gate, hit the right color buoy, follow paths, and drop markers in specified bins. My emotion came from being one of two high school teams that made the finals in a field of 31 teams. I was glad that my contributions with JKBotz were paying off.

My interest in robotics began when my dad frequently took me to robotics conventions in Silicon Valley, where I grew up. Companies displayed robots made from Legos to humanoids. The possibilities presented in these conventions fascinated me so I purchased a standard Lego Mindstorms robotics kit in middle school to experiment with. I then joined a middle school robotics team where most of my teammates also had Lego robotics at home, so we worked together to win intra-school competitions. We were the giants then, and I kept this mentality of achievement into high school when I joined a new field of robotics and a new team. However, I soon realized that the level of robotics at JKBotz was at a much higher caliber than what I had worked with in middle school. At JKBotz, building an autonomous submarine was much more complex than building from robot Lego kits. Another hurdle was that in JKBotz, funding for expensive parts and advice was not readily available. In this environment, teamwork was crucial to compensate for these shortfalls.

To prepare for RoboSub, we needed new members with diverse skills: electrical, software, and mechanical. In addition to working on Barracuda, each member had to function as a team to get the materials and educate members. I had to fundraise (raised about $2,500) by writing grants and presenting our sub at community events. As a team we had to spend long hours during the school year and almost everyday of summer in a member's garage to build on our progress. These extra efforts made our finals position in RoboSub much more rewarding.

All these experiences now came full circle as I was heading to the hotel pool with the sub to test new software fixes before going to the competition site for the final event. At this point we were already overwhelmed by the fact that we made it to the final rounds and just wanted to fix any possible problems. Members started to mobilize and work on different tasks, even if the job was out of their specific field. I was proud to work with and represent this dedicated and still developing team as their input, ideas, spirit, and determination made this memorable event possible. With JKBotz, I developed my programming skills for robotics, and most importantly, saw how working as a team can make my interests more gratifying. It is these experiences that made we wonder what I can achieve with persistence to pursue my passions, and by sticking with groups that share my enthusiasm.

Tyler's final draft starts off with him receiving a tweet! Already the reader is engaged in his interest in technology. By giving his submarine a name, Tyler easily draws us into the world of robotics, explaining its features and the tricks he tries to get the Barracuda to perform. Tyler did a great job of making engineering exciting. We're left not only impressed with his coding skills, but we've learned about the importance of teamwork in the engineering field.

Discuss an accomplishment or event, formal or informal, that marked your transition from childhood to adulthood within your culture, community, or family.

"Anyohaseyo, anyohaseyo," chanted one of the residents at Amber Gardens Senior Communities, as she enthusiastically waved goodbye to all the children. When she first arrived at the beading class hosted by our organization at the assisted living unit, Sara complained about being the only person of Korean descent at the center. By the time she left, however, long after I had spoken to her in the little Korean I knew, she was decked out in a rainbow sea creature necklace she made with Suhavi, a yellow star bracelet made for her by Nivaaz, and a huge smile from interacting with the kids. And she wasn't the only one. When we left at noon, all the residents were heartily thanking us and begging for us to revisit.

As a child, I always had a passion for service, wanting to share my compassion with others. For example, in fourth grade, my friend and I harnessed our love for animals by organizing a school-wide drive for the Humane Society. In seventh grade, I returned the UGG boots I had been dreaming of for Christmas because I found out they were made of animal fur, and later I became fully vegan. Beyond my personal crusade against animal cruelty in particular, I've always been excited to help out in the community in many ways, whether it be through my daily habits or my extensive volunteer work.

By the end of sophomore year, however, I decided I needed to challenge myself by taking on a more adult role, expanding my desire to give back to the community. I wanted to move past being a volunteer to sharing my passion for service. In other words, I wanted to move past writing a spoken word poem about "pledging to go without fur" in my creative writing class to teaching younger kids how to change the lives of animals in need. I wanted to move past dutifully fulfilling the instructions from my supervisor at the Stanford Blood Center to inspiring kids like Saanvi and Pari to warm Sara's heart at Amber Gardens and sharing opportunities for them to take action themselves.

That's why I, in collaboration with my sister, started Kids for Causes. And now, I can confidently say that I have transitioned from a childhood role as a volunteer to an adult role as a leader, creating a unique way to garner interest in volunteerism in my community. Our morning beading class at Amber Gardens marked the last volunteering activity of the week for all of the kids attending our 2013 summer camp. Saanvi and Pari were two of the seven year olds who participated for the second year in a row. Besides visiting the elderly at Amber Gardens, they wrote letters to soldiers via A Million Thanks, put together school packages in cloth bags they decorated for UMCOR, and volunteered at the Full Circle Sunshine Garden, amongst other activities. As I watch their enthusiasm for charitable activities like these grow, I am excited to organize more and more events for young children in my community to help others out.

On one level, it is extremely gratifying to hear a representative from the Humane Society tell us they "are so grateful for the blankets and toys [the kids] made and donated" and that their "cats and kittens will benefit greatly from the donation of these items," or to receive from Karen Walter of Angel Food "a BIG thank you to the big hearted kids at Kids for Causes for contributing thirty homemade and hand-decorated bag lunches to kids in two apartment buildings and to folks waiting to turn in cans at the local recycling center." However, I get the greatest sense of fulfillment from hearing kids beseech me to organize another volunteering event soon or regale me with stories from when they revisited an organization we worked with. That's when I know that I've moved from making a difference myself to affecting a far greater impact by becoming a leader, influencing others to enjoy service just as much as I do.

COMMENTS:

- Start off with a visual of you preparing the children for their service project.

- Define your role more clearly at the start.

- What challenges did you have motivating students or helping them feel comfortable with strangers?

- How is your organization different than Scouts or other groups that provide community service?

{ KEIKO—FINAL DRAFT }

Twelve eager-eyed elementary-schoolers gathered around me in my backyard. The

Giving Book *lay open, and I'd accounted for every detail. However, I wanted everything to go right at our first event two summers ago at Kids for Causes, where we'd kick off the week-long program with readings, introductions, arts-and-crafts activities, and acts of volunteering. My sister and I started this organization to promote social awareness and volunteerism amongst children, and I was ready to embrace my adult role as a leader. So I brushed aside any lingering self-doubt and enthusiastically began, "Who can tell me about giving and charity?"*

Sophomore year, I decided to expand my desire to contribute to the community from my direct volunteering during my childhood, to teaching younger kids how to positively impact others' lives by founding Kids for Causes. Rather than applying for a position at an existing program, I wanted to personally select organizations that could most benefit from my young volunteers' vibrancy and to specifically shape our activities towards the organizations' needs. Local chapters of Scouts or the YMCA do exist with overlapping goals regarding service; however, my organization is unique in its coed, low-cost, low-commitment nature. We also don't use badges—all rewards are intrinsic.

Organizing our first program required advertising, planning activities, organizing locations for service, purchasing supplies, arranging for adult supervisors to help chaperone, and enhancing the website. None of these tasks surmounted to the ultimate challenge – actually channeling the kids' energy towards volunteerism once our week of activities began. At Amber Gardens Senior Communities, I conferred with the volunteer director to arrange a visit that would best utilize the kids' fun personalities to benefit the residents. We decided on a trivia game, a cooking class, and a talent show. I thought I'd prepared the kids for the day through readings, a discussion relating giving and charity to working with the elderly, and extensive practice of the talent show. However, upon arrival, the kids, who had just been enthusiastically practicing their rendition of a catchy song called "Saving Polar Bears" during the ride over, suddenly became extremely shy. Nervously smiling, they hid behind me when meeting the residents, many of whom suffered from speech-hampering disabilities or chronic illnesses. However, as I encouraged them, helped them wheel the residents into an activity room, and started the trivia game, they began happily talking with the seniors. Because the biggest struggle the kids faced was simply lacking comfort in interacting with older people they'd never met, even just modeling for them to talk about school or to ask the residents about their favorite foods eased apprehension. As the children followed me in starting conversations with the residents, the kids' behaviors became natural, and I could see them relaxing as they mingled with everyone there. By the time the kids performed the talent show for the delighted seniors, no one wanted to say goodbye. It was so gratifying to see not only how ecstatic the residents were, but also how happy the kids became as volunteers.

I love receiving heartfelt thank-you notes from the eight non-profits we've served so far. As I plan more events, it's amazing to watch our outreach expand and have reverberating effects both locally and globally – most recently when we decorated and packaged school supply kits for vulnerable communities in conflict zones across the globe via UMCOR, a humanitarian relief organization. However, I feel the greatest fulfillment from kids beseeching me to organize another volunteering event or regaling me with stories from when they revisited an organization that we aided on their own. That's when I can confidently say that I've achieved my goal and moved from making a difference myself to accomplishing a far greater impact by embracing an adult role as a leader, creating a unique way to garner interest in volunteerism and influencing others to enjoy service as much as I do.

Keiko's essay originally focused too much on the organizations she was involved with and far less on her as a role model with responsibilities both to the children who were in her program and the recipients of her charitable work. Starting the essay with a "visual" of her surrounded by children immediately draws the reader in. She also makes it clearer why she started her organization and how it is different from other youth programs. She keeps the focus on herself and the youth group rather than confusing the reader with the names and stories of people she met while volunteering. We get to know Keiko more as a leader in this final draft.

CONCLUSION

In season five of *Modern Family*, sixteen-year-old Alex Dunphy schedules herself an appointment with a therapist. Crushed by endless study for the SAT and overloaded with coursework for AP classes, Alex can no longer cope with the stress of being a high school student and worrying about college admission. When Alex tells her parents she's taking the bus alone to her first therapy appointment, her father whispers to her mother, "She's like a self-cleaning oven." The world, unfortunately, has convinced teens like Alex and their parents that getting into college is a stoic exercise to be done without help. But, high-achieving as she is, Alex, too, needs a mentor.

The writing of this book was prompted by many factors—including my own experiences with two daughters navigating their way through high school. True in all families, siblings are unique individuals. One daughter fit in seamlessly in high school with great self-confidence and many friends—a natural leader. She won many awards at graduation, and admission to many fine colleges was expected by teachers who knew her well. My other daughter, equally bright and talented, never fit into the mainstream of public high school life. Her interests, leadership, and creativity were off the radar of the school's faculty. She left school every day at 2 p.m. to take a bus, then a train, for an hour-and-a-half long journey alone into the city, where she began her training in theatre directing and dramaturgy with a highly acclaimed professional acting company. She was never in a school play; the high school drama teacher never even met her. When she was admitted to her dream college, two faculty members and an administrator asked her, "Why did they take *you*?" Those comments summed up how little they knew her.

The college essay, I believe, was an opportunity for both my daughters to reveal what others had not seen. For one, writing the essay allowed her to explore her fear of failure; she wrestled with what might happen if her imperfections were discovered. Her essay allowed the colleges to see behind the stellar report card and letters of recommendation to appreciate a multi-dimensional young woman who had struggled to keep it all together—whose world was not as neat and tidy as it appeared on the surface. For my other daughter, the challenge of preparing the college essay allowed her to write about her artistic process—an opportunity never given to her in the classroom, but one which occupied her thoughts and imagination during the entire course of her high school experience. I am sure her essay added a critical dimension to her application, revealing insights that the letters of recommendation from her calculus and Spanish teachers could not. Her essay also provided the context and validation, I believe, for the letter of recommendation from her artistic director that was submitted along with her academic recommendations. That letter was later shared with me: "She is not a bundle of sparks," it read. "She is in medium gear pushing a thread of inspiration forward off the main road, quietly determined and undeterred with a twinkle in her eye, knowing she just might have something unusual to offer the world."

This book, I hope, will give mentors increased empathy for those college applicants (most of them) who enter this process with trepidation. I encourage you to delight in the journey you are about to enter with a student—to be a partner in this path of self-exploration. Regardless of whether your students are admitted to the colleges of their dreams, the essays they will write will be an important moment in their lives and a testament to what it means to be a teen in the early twenty-first century.

APPENDIX 1–FULL VERSIONS OF SAMPLES OF COMMON APPLICATION ESSAYS

Some students have a background or story that is so central to their identity that they believe their application would be incomplete without it. If this sounds like you, then please share your story.

Whenever I walk into a Chinese restaurant with my family, we're one of the many Chinese-American families waiting to be seated among the cramped tables to eat pork buns or bowls of steaming congee. But when one of the waiters notices my family, he or she inevitably asks us "Ji wei?" No matter how many times my family of four is asked this simple question, our response is always the same: we stare blankly at the waiter before holding up four fingers.

One might think that, as an Asian kid growing up in the Bay Area (where nearly every fourth person is of Asian descent), I would fit in perfectly fine; however, living in California means I'm surrounded every day by first-generation Chinese-Americans who may superficially resemble me but are otherwise vastly different. My public school celebrates Chinese New Year, but my family doesn't distribute red envelopes and never goes to the annual San Francisco Chinese New Year parade. I've never been to China; I travel to Boston or New Orleans to see my relatives, not Taipei or Hong Kong. My mom cooks spaghetti more often than fried rice. Most importantly, my parents never forced me to attend Chinese School.

Neither my parents nor I were ever taught Chinese as children. However, while I grew up in the Bay Area, they grew up in areas where to be Chinese was to be an outsider. My mom was forbidden from learning Chinese My mother's parents fled the growing number of Chinese communists and consequently loathed anything that reminded them of China, including the language. My father's parents spoke different dialects of Chinese, and the language was never spoken in their household.

My parents may have decided to raise a family in California in order to distance me from the racial prejudices of their hometowns, but being Chinese-American while not fully understanding Chinese language and culture has made me feel disconnected from my heritage. And so, when I got the chance to take Chinese in high school, I did, and found that Chinese was possibly the most difficult language I could have chosen. The similar-looking characters, the pronunciations that my mouth wasn't used to making, and the complex hieroglyphics that I had to write, all made for a seemingly impossible language to learn.

However, studying Chinese rather than speaking it at home has forced me to take a closer look at what it is about culture that I value. To be honest, I'm not sure what drives me to pursue Chinese fluency; perhaps it's my love for my rare family dinners involving so many enticing (and weird) Chinese dishes, my desire to reconnect with my heritage, or my appreciation for the beauty of the Chinese language. Nor do I know where my study of Chinese language will take me. Maybe I'll find my grand-parents' birthplaces, study abroad in China, or order a Chinese meal. However, that doesn't matter; for the time being, I may not yet be able to read the menu at a Chinese restaurant or a read a Chinese newspaper, but when asked "Ji wei?" I'm proud to now be able to answer "Si wei."

Recount an incident or time when you experienced failure. How did it affect you, and what lessons did you learn?

The greatest failure I have ever experienced was when I did not get first chair in my school orchestra. Later, I realized that my failure was really only a disappointment and I was able to come out of the situation stronger. In my orchestra, the first chairs are student leaders who help manage their musical section. It is an honor to be a first chair because of the caliber of our orchestra, which earned unanimous superiors last year at the Musical Education Association competition.

In my section, violin, there is one student who sits in the first chair who has responsi-bilities such as taking attendance, relaying messages from the conductor, and passing out new music. I wanted to be chosen as first chair to show how much passion I had for the orchestra and to be a role model for the other musicians. Throughout all my time in the program, but especially during my junior year, I practiced a lot so that I would be good enough to be the first chair violinist. I also tried to act as a leader even without the title, and demonstrate to my conductor, who picks the first chairs, that I would be able to lead my section. Towards the end of the year I thought that I showed my true ability and potential and I knew I did everything that I could to prove that my conductor should chose me. In the spring of my junior year the conduc-tor announced that it was time to audition for the first chair positions for the coming year. I was really excited because I was sure I would be chosen.

At the end-of-the-year banquet the new first chairs would be announced. Each musical section was called to the front of the room so that the graduating first chairs could announce the new ones. I confidently went up to the front of the room, with my violin section, and I felt betrayed and humiliated when the name I heard announced was not mine. I felt personally insulted in front of the entire orchestra, parents, volunteers, and staff. As soon as I understood my dream was lost I was just upset and I wanted to quit orchestra all together because I thought it was too embarrassing that I did not get the position. At this point I was only concerned with my own success and I am sure my fellow musicians had similar goals and were trying just as hard as I was to become first chair. It was not fair for me to just overlook everyone else's efforts and have that feeling of entitlement.

As time went by I realized the lesson I learned from this experience was that being a leader does not mean having a title. I know that during my senior year, I can put my three years of orchestra experience to good use and help my section regardless. Looking back, not being chosen as first chair is more of a disappointment than a failure. I did my best and I really tried in every possible way to get the position I aspired for. My goal was really just to help my orchestra which I will surely still be able to do in my final year of playing with my section.

Reflect on a time when you challenged a belief or idea. What prompted you to act? Would you make the same decision again?

"Don't cry, Alice," I said to myself as I gripped my pen tightly and scribbled on my notebook. Larry sat across from me on his musky leather couch, grabbing tissues to wipe the tears falling down from his face as he remembered the fateful night of November 4, 2008, the night that California passed Proposition 8, the ballot measure that illegalized same-sex marriages and possibly nullified existing marriages between same-sex couples, like that of Larry and his husband. I kept willing myself not to cry, trying to remain a completely professional journalist, but I felt a few tears forming in my eyes. I smiled as I thought about how strange this situation was: here I was, crying with a fifty-year-old man whom I had just met five minutes ago.

I had come to interview Larry and his family for my story in the school newsmagazine on Proposition 8 and its effects on the gay- and lesbian-headed households at my school. I had read many newspaper articles about Proposition 8, but none of *the stories I had read had detailed the psychological effects on the families and the children of these gay and lesbian couples who were caught in the middle of a huge political battle.*

I had always taken for granted the basic right I have: the right to say that my parents were married. My parents will never worry about having hospital visitation rights because they are married under the law— and have the right to marry because they are heterosexual.

I spent months writing and rewriting my story, ripping up draft after draft because none of them did the families justice. Sometimes I got so frustrated that I just sat on my bed, staring at my computer screen with all of my interviews typed up. But I could not keep myself away from telling the families' stories, the stories of long-awaited weddings and exasperating legal battles. I had to set aside the politics of the issue and tell their stories and show others what they had shown me: that love can truly conquer all. My story was not about gay rights or homosexuality; it was about people fighting for equality. With this in mind, I cranked out the final version of the story in one night.

My story received feedback from all corners of the continent, from Idaho to Canada. Most of the comments praised me for revealing a new perspective on the gay rights issue; however, there were a few that put down the families and accused me of being a "homo-lover," as one man put it. But what kind of journalist would I be if I succumbed to these insults and shied away from reporting on important issues just because of what a few people thought? Writing this article made me realize that my words and my actions can give any underrepresented group of people the power to share their stories. I've continued writing about issues that matter to me, from Muslim students struggling to fit in at a secular school to lower-income students trying to excel academically in an impoverished school community. Every time I report on a new issue, the stories of the families who I interviewed for my Proposition 8 story remain in the back of my mind, reminding me of the impact that I can have on others.

Despite the fact that California had voted against his marriage, Larry remained hopeful for a different future where all families like his could call themselves families. Writing this story opened my eyes to all people who have felt misjudged or discriminated against. Larry's passion for his cause inspired me to continue learning about different people and shedding light on issues that others disregard. As a journalist, I will continue sharing the stories of those whose voices have been silenced; as a person, I will continue fighting for the civil liberties of the underdogs in the world.

Discuss an accomplishment or event, formal or informal, that marked your transition from childhood to adulthood within your culture, community, or family.

I was waiting for a young woman, Linda, to come out of the shower at the Coalition for Homeless Youth where I volunteer every week. I sat in my usual metal chair outside of the shower room. The clipboard with the list of names of the people lined up for the shower rested on my lap, along with the timer. When the timer went off, I knocked on the door for Linda to come out. Linda walked out of the shower wearing a colorful skirt, slightly torn at the hem, and a white blouse. I was confused because I wasn't used to seeing someone come out of the shower in clean clothes. She was smiling as she was putting on a little make up so I asked her what was the occasion. She told me that today was her wedding day. I was so surprised and amazed that someone from the homeless population of Chicago was going to be married. She had needed the shower to do what most brides do on their wedding day—get ready. Except Linda did not have any hair stylists or family to help her get ready, she only had herself and the small amount of products that we offered to the homeless youth. Despite her situation, Linda lit up the entire space with her excitement. As I watched her talk to the other homeless participants about her wedding, I couldn't help but think, is it possible for a homeless person to experience happiness? Before I started volunteering at the Coalition for Homeless Youth, I never imagined that a homeless person could be happy. I saw them as mentally unstable, drug-addicted, depressed people. Linda's story combined with many other experiences that I've seen homeless youth experiencing joy and other day-to-day emotions, changed my perception of homeless people. I realized that it didn't matter that Linda had spent years living on the streets because marriage doesn't have to do with material belongings. She was in love and could experience joy just like anyone else.

After months of working in the showers handing out towels, I was promoted to an outreach volunteer. Because I had shown my commitment to this kind of social work, the founder of the Coalition allowed me to join the staff on outreach. This opportunity was my transition to taking on adult responsibilities in my volunteer community.

Every week I walk West Roosevelt with two other outreach workers and we hand out snacks and hygiene supplies to homeless youth. We can never know if a homeless youth is dangerous, or strung out or even ill, still we offer them our services because we are not ones to judge their lifestyle. By encountering strangers on the street and having no conception as to what mental state they're in, I have learned to go out of my comfort zone. Now I walk West Roosevelt without judging anyone based on what they look like or what state they are in.

Describe a place or environment where you are perfectly content. What do you do or experience there, and why is it meaningful to you?

My alarm blares at 4:00 a.m. every Thursday morning.

I roll myself out of bed fortified by the knowledge that I'm not the only one getting up at this absurd hour. Sleepy and grumpy, I pull on my rowing gear, wolf down some cereal, grab my backpack and head out.

I do enjoy the quiet of the predawn chill and darkness. By 5:00 a.m., I'm at the boathouse at the Brittingham Boathouse on Monona Bay in Madison. As more rowers arrive, the chatter picks up and I start to feel excited about getting onto the water.

I'm truly content after a satisfying workout with my team. When all the rowers seated in my boat are present, I feel motivated. It's a demanding fifteen-hour per week practice schedule, so I really respect the other rowers who, along with me, have stuck with it over the past three years. We'll work together to have a fast morning on the water.

At six feet four inches, I fit right in with this lanky bunch. At the coxswain's command, all eight of us methodically convene around our sleek boat and heave her onto our shoulders. We carry her onto the wobbly dock and gently lower her into the lake. Our coxswain instructs us to step carefully into the boat together, one foot at a time.

Seated, I catch my blade into the cold water, but feel uncomfortably offbeat. It's time to find my rhythm with the team, so I watch the rower in front of me before dipping in again.

After about fifteen minutes of lightly paced rowing, my muscles warm and strengthen;

my pull becomes fluid. I move more precisely in synch with the group; one beat to take a stroke, three beats to roll up the slide. Compressing my long body, I catch my blade into the water and push back hard with my legs before pulling the oar securely toward me. All eight blades glide gracefully just above the water, before diving down to make another crisp catch. Subtle hand and body positions influence efficiency, so each stroke taken together is impeccably choreographed. The effort builds as we pick up speed. I'm breathing hard now as we start to tear through the water. It's thrilling!

True contentment comes after rowing with my team at maximum force, with clear focus and precise technique. I know I'm giving my all because it hurts. On race day, when we're neck-and-neck with our rival teams, it's this precision, efficiency, power, stamina and grit that give us the winning edge.

I'm a confident rower now, but haven't always been, of course. A classmate introduced me to crew during freshman year. I was willing to try something new.

Even as an awkward beginner, I knew immediately I was in the right place, with the right people. I'd swum competitively for years, so adapted easily to the aerobic demands of rowing. Unlike swimming, however, rowing provided a team dynamic much more interesting to me than the monotony of staring at the bottom of a pool. Swimming emphasizes individual accomplishment, but success in rowing comes only when each rower fully commits to the success of the boat.

I'm passionate about making a success of any group that I'm a part of, and drawn to those who offer the same enthusiasm. Whether it's a medal-winning boat, school presentation, summer office job, or family conflict, I like being in groups in which the work of being a member builds the community, and the community supports the individuals within it. During a race, my powerful strokes are essential to making the boat fast, but so is every stroke of every other rower.

It's humbling to know I can't always accomplish something alone and inspiring to know I don't always have to.

STUDENT QUESTIONNAIRE

Name _____ Date _____

Date of birth _____ Email address _____ Cell # _____

The goal is to think about the factors or qualities that will make your college years exciting, fun, and full of new experiences. The task is to identify, at least initially, those factors that will fulfill your goals. As you go through this process, you may find questions you have not yet considered or are uncertain about. This is just a place to start!

Have you ever looked at a college website? _____

Do you have ideas about courses you would like to take? _____

_____

_____

_____

Some schools have a very rigid set of requirements and some let you have lots of choices. Do you have a preference for one or the other? _____

_____

_____

_____

Do you know what a MAJOR and MINOR are? _____
Have you considered a MAJOR? _____

(You don't usually have to declare a major until your junior year–so it's fine if you don't know yet!)

EXTRACURRICULAR ACTIVITIES

What are your current activities (sports, music, robotics, work, etc.) outside of school or at school? _____

_____

_____

_____

Which of your current interests do you want to continue in college? _____

_____

_____

_____

What activities might you want to try? _____

_____

_____

_____

What is your first language? _____

What language do you speak at home? _____

Has your schooling been disrupted for illnesses, suspensions, academic issues? _____

If so, please briefly explain. _____

_____

_____

_____

Do you receive additional academic support at school? _____

If so, briefly explain. _____
_____
_____
_____

Do you receive additional academic support outside of school, for test preparation or with tutors? _____

If so, briefly explain. _____
_____
_____
_____

What states have you traveled to? _____
_____
_____
_____

Have you traveled outside of the country? _____

If so, where and when? _____
_____
_____
_____

At home, what do you and your parent(s) tend to agree on? _____

_____

_____

_____

At home, what do you and your parent(s) tend to disagree about? _____

_____

_____

_____

List any colleges you have visited and when: _____

_____

_____

_____

APPENDIX 3–PARENT QUESTIONNAIRE

PARENT QUESTIONNAIRE

Student Name: _____ Date: _____

Parent name(s): _____

Student lives with: _____ both parents _____ mother _____ father _____ other

Home address: _____

Home telephone: _____ Cell: _____

Email address(es): _____

Student date of birth: _____ Current grade: _____

Present school: _____ Dates: _____

Previous schools attended: _____

_____

_____

_____

Siblings (names, grade levels, schools or colleges attended): _____

_____

_____

_____

Parent 1

Occupation: _____ Highest degree earned: _____

College(s) attended: _____

Parent 2

Occupation: _____ Highest degree earned: _____

College(s) attended: _____

What is your current level of satisfaction with your student's present school? What works and/or doesn't work there? Why did you choose this particular school?_____

_____

_____

_____

Can you comment on your student's level of self-esteem and confidence? _____

_____

_____

_____

What are the major areas of agreement or disagreement between you and your scholar?

_____

_____

_____

_____

What can you list as your student's academic strengths and weaknesses:

Strengths: _____

_____

_____

_____

Weaknesses: _____

_____

_____

_____

What are your expectations regarding the college experience for your scholar?

    a.   Academic: _____

    b.   Social and Personal: _____

    c.   Career: _____

Imagine that you are writing your student's recommendation. What has your student accomplished in the past? How do you think teachers perceive your student? _____

_____

_____

_____

What classroom or testing accommodations seem to help your student best? Is s/he able to advocate for his/her own needs? _____

_____

_____

_____

What are the primary questions you have for me?_____

_____

_____

_____

APPENDIX 4–RÉSUMÉ TEMPLATE

Résumé Template

Your Name

Address, City, State, Zip

Phone number, e-mail

EDUCATION

Clinton High School *(private, public, parochial)*

San Francisco, CA

• Will graduate in June 2015

• 3.56 unweighted GPA, 3.86 weighted GPA

Senior year courses (Fall 2014)

• SAT Reasoning

• SAT Subject

• AP Scores (if applicable)

• ACT (if applicable)

HONORS AND AWARDS

• Received Clinton High Math Award (2012).

• Received Honorable Mention in San Francisco Art Institute's "Young Film Talent" show.

• Fourth place finish, Lincoln-Douglas debate, Bay Area High School Debate Regional Tournament (2013).

ACTIVITIES AND LEADERSHIP

Clinton High School Debate Club: Founder and President *(2012-present)*
San Francisco, CA
• Founded debate club at Clinton High. Coordinated with president of Convent of Sacred Heart debate to form co-ed team. Attracted 26 members in first year. Managed training and practice schedule.
• Lincoln-Douglas debater. Team finished sixth overall in region (2013).

Pacific Medical Center: Junior Volunteer *(2010-present)*
San Francisco, CA
• Over 300 volunteer hours to date.
• Train 20 new incoming Junior Volunteers each year.
• Member of selection committee for new Junior Volunteer candidates.
• Coordinated children's book drive to create a library of 350 books.
• Created and organized first annual talent show for the Pacific Retirement Home.
• Coordinator of Pediatric Center Valentine and Thanksgiving decorations.
• Red Cross CPR certified.

Clinton Varsity Basketball Team: Member *(2012-present)*
San Francisco, CA
• Point guard.
• Team finished 4th in league despite lack of senior players (2013).

WORK AND SUMMER EXPERIENCE

Insight Management Resources *(2011-present)*
San Bruno, CA
• Marketing Intern. Assist Director of Marketing in creating new client database.

Cornell University Summer College Research Apprenticeship Program *(2012)*
Ithaca, NY
• Program accepts three students each year to conduct scientific research with a professor.
• Conducted research under Dr. Praveen Salaam on using lentiviral vectors for gene therapy of Beta-Thalassemia. Results contributed to Dr. Salaam's forthcoming article (June, 2015) in *The Journal of Gene Therapy.*

Putney Student Travel Language Immersion Program in France *(2011)*
France
• Spent six weeks traveling through the country and staying with a family in Nice.

LANGUAGES

Fluent in Cantonese, proficient in French.

HOBBIES

Rock climbing, hiking, bug collecting, and making short films.

ACKNOWLEDGEMENTS

With special thanks to the student writers who generously contributed to this book:

Amelia Alvarez	Ronald Patrick Lynch
Meha Bakshi	Sam Maller
Talia Bornstein	Reyna McKinnon
Ava Burton	Ashwin Mehta
Anmol Chadha	Margot Pierluissi
Doria E. Charlson	Sarah Pierluissi
Meredith Joelle Charlson	Joshua Pitkofsky
Gilly Dosovitsky	Andrew Rosenzweig
Alexandra Dwyer	Alijah Rubin
Matthew Hargadon	Karan Samel
Nadine Herman	Isabelle Smith
John Herrera	Alana Sobel
Max Herrera	Angela Solis
Gabriel Hoffman	Garrett Tan
Phillip Hoxie	Amanda Young
Charles Kellenberger	

Many thanks also to my editor at Wintergreen Orchard House, Stephanie Farah, for her enthusiasm, encouragement, and helpful suggestions. To Anne Zimmerman, who mentored me through the conceptualization of this book. To Rachel Barany, a "secret reader," for her insights, wisdom, and great humor. To the University of California, Berkeley, Extension Certificate Program in College Admissions and Career Planning for the opportunity to develop and teach the course on the college essay. To a long lost pen pal who told me I could be a writer.

NOTES

Chapter 1

1 http://www.nces.ed.gov/programs/coe/indicator_coi.asp.

2 Jerome Karabel, The Chosen: *The Hidden History of Admission and Exclusion at Harvard, Yale, and Princeton* (New York: Houghton Mifflin, 2005).

Chapter 3

3 Dan McAdams, *The Stories We Live: Personal Myths and the Making of the Self* (New York: The Guilford Press, 1997).

4 John D. Mayer, "Three levels of knowing a person," *Psychology Today* (November 8, 2010), accessed July 1, 2014, http://www.psychologytoday.com/blog/the-personality-analyst/201011/three-levels-knowing-person.

5 Margarita Tartakovsky, "The Power of Stories in Personality Psychology," *Psych Central* (2011), accessed June 16, 2014, http://psychcentral.com/lib/the-power-of-stories-in-personal-psychology/0008589.

6 Sam Gosling, *Snoop: What Your Stuff Says About You* (New York: Basic Books, 2008).

7 Phillip Lopate, "The Essay, an Exercise in Doubt," *The New York Times* (January 28, 2013), accessed July 1, 2014, http://opinionator.blogs.nytimes.com/2013/02/16/the-essay-an-exercise-in-doubt/?_php=true&_type=blogs&_r=0.

Chapter 4

8 *A Prairie Home Companion*, American Public Media.

9 Justice Sonia Sotomayor, interview by Michael Krasny, *Forum with Michael Krasny*, podcast audio, January 28, 2013, http://www.kqed.org/a/forum/R201301281000.

10 Sonia Sotomayor, *My Beloved World* (New York: Knopf, 2013).

Chapter 7

11 *Amadeus*, dir. by Milos Forman (1984; Warner Home Video, 1997 dvd).

Chapter 8

12 Betty Hart, Todd Risley, *Meaningful Differences in the Everyday Experiences of American Children* (Baltimore: Paul H. Brooks Publishing Co., 1995).

13 Teresa Cherry-Cruz, "Enhancing Literacy Through the Techniques of Storytelling," *The ASHA Leader* (December 26, 2001), accessed July 1, 2014, http://www.asha.org/Publications/leader/2001/011226/storytelling.htm.

14 "Malcolm Gladwell Live from the Castro," 3200 Stories, podcast audio, October 8, 2013, http://www.3200stories.org/blog/post/malcolm-gladwell-live-from-the-castro.

Chapter 9

15 National Association for College Admission Counseling, *Report of the Commission on International Student Recruitment* (May 2013), accessed July 1, 2014, http://www.insidehighered.com/sites/default/server_files/files/NACAC International Commission Report_Pre-Pub Draft.pdf.

16 University of California office of the President, accessed July 1, 2014, http://www.ucop.edu/newss/factssheets/2014.